A GRAND

ILLUSION

How Progressive Christianity
Undermines Biblical Faith

REVISED & EXPANDED

DAVID YOUNG

To Joanne, Gerald, Don, Nancy, and Bob. May this book honor your encouragement. And to Gloria, who loved the sacred Scriptures.

Contents

REN∃W

RENEWING THE TEACHINGS OF JESUS
TO FUEL DISCIPLE MAKING

Introduction

I am flawed on many obvious levels, and truthfully, I erroneously report my zip code at least two out of every ten times. So why would I write about pursuing a rich understanding of the Bible? Isn't that material reserved for the upper echelon of the church hierarchy? The ones who have "arrived"? The answer is fundamental: the insights of the Bible are not reserved for pastors, their wives, and Billy Graham. Psalm 119:130, one of the most beautiful passages concerning God's Word, says, "The unfolding of your words gives light; it gives understanding to the simple."

—Jen Hatmaker[1]

It is possible that, until recently, nearly half of America's evangelical world had never heard of Jen Hatmaker—even though millions of evangelicals have been encouraged by her warm, relaxed, and relatable blogs and books for years. Her books routinely outsell those of popular authors such as T. D. Jakes and Max Lucado, and her books have landed on the *New York Times* Best Sellers list multiple times. She often speaks to sold-out crowds, she has nearly a million followers on Twitter and Facebook, and podcast listeners stream her content around the world.

Those who had never heard of her were, of course, male evangelicals. As a group, evangelical males read less than their female counterparts, and when they do read, evangelical males tend toward more institutional authors such as pastors and ministry leaders. Hatmaker's popularity is more democratic. Like so many other women evangelical leaders who have not been afforded the same institutional options, Hatmaker won her many followers on the open range of the Internet.

In 2016, however, nearly every evangelical man learned Hatmaker's name—in fact, the entire U.S. woke up to hear of Jen Hatmaker. Bucking the evangelical consensus on the subject of gender and sexuality in 2016, Hatmaker made national news when she announced her support of LGBT relationships. After developing friendships with several gays and lesbians and subsequently reconsidering what the Bible says, Jen Hatmaker announced to the world her conclusion that same-sex relationships are biblical and holy.

Other evangelical leaders had come out in favor of LGBT relationships, but Hatmaker seemed different. That's because Hatmaker is so warm and likeable, much like a big sister or a trusted friend, and so enormously popular, that many simply could not ignore her new stance. Many evangelicals applauded Hatmaker and joined her in support of LGBT unions. For them Hatmaker is a hero—they delight to snap a selfie with her at events such as the Wild Goose Festival and check one off their bucket list. How can someone so winsome, so attractive, and so loving be so wrong? For other evangelicals, however, Hatmaker's announcement brought great sadness and dismay. Conservative Southern evangelicals were forced to restate their positions on sex. Lifeway bookstores stopped carrying her books. Many evangelicals mourned another concession to America's secular values.

Whole churches found themselves having to make difficult decisions about Hatmaker's material: Should their members use her books and attend her conferences? Even families found themselves divided and unable to talk about Hatmaker—just the mention of her name unleashed deeply held passions that could wreck a family dinner.

Evidence of a Seismic Shift

Jen Hatmaker's announcement is not an isolated change in one person's thinking. It's bigger than that: it signifies a seismic shift happening in evangelicalism today. Her new views on sex have exposed a deep and seemingly impassible divide emerging among North American Christians—a divide in the name of sex, yes, but a divide that has to do with much more than sex.

It is somewhat odd that a formerly private thing such as sex has become the dividing line between traditional Christians and progressives in

North America—but it has indeed. In America, sex is both nothing and everything.[2] It is nothing in that the emerging American consensus seems to be that very few sex and gender rules exist. Sex is, well, just sex—it's no big deal. But sex is also everything in the U.S. because it has become a major religious, cultural, and political battleground. Sex is everywhere, and people are no longer allowed to remain silent about what they believe with regard to sex and gender in America. Sex is the defining issue of our day. It is everything.

Much deeper questions lie behind the arguments about sex and gender among Christians: How will we decide what constitutes the Christian faith and what does not? What is our ultimate authority in Christianity? And in which direction does Christianity point—backward to the work of the apostles and prophets, or forward to the vision of progress prominent in North America?

For more than a century and a half, North American Protestants have clashed over these questions.

On the right stand those who believe that the apostolic witness as preserved for us in the Scriptures and interpreted for us by the major creeds and confessions has the final say in what constitutes the Christian faith. The desire to be faithful to historic Christianity has defined this group, which, over the last hundred years, has frequently been labeled "evangelical," although numerous other groups also hold to the authority of Scriptures and historic Christianity (including the massive Roman Catholic Church, Orthodox churches, Charismatic churches, most Community churches, and others).

On the left stand those who believe that, though the Bible is one source for the Christian faith, there are other sources—often better sources—such as social science, psychology, recent theories of justice, and even sentimentality. Since the American Civil War, such Christians have typically borne either the label "liberal" or "progressive."[3]

In recent years, many evangelicals have begun to shift from their once strongly-held position on the final authority of Scripture toward a more progressive vision of the faith—one that is often built on sentiment and in general step with secular values. This shift toward theological progressivism is growing in size, fueled by the emergence of a vast theory of social justice that defines the work of Jesus in terms of inclusiveness, self-actualization, identity politics, and the like.

Nothing represents this divide quite like sex, which is one of America's most-worshiped gods. Big-name evangelical leaders (or formerly evangelical leaders) have sought to redefine Christian theology so as to approve of same-sex behavior, transgenderism, and the like. It's not just Hatmaker. Rob Bell has long argued that biblical sexual ethics were backward and oppressive. Ten years ago, Brian McLaren called for a "moratorium" on discussions about same-sex behavior, before he then performed a same-sex wedding and threw his support behind it. Even Tony Campolo, who famously opposed same-sex activity as un-Christian, announced that he had changed his mind as he approached his eightieth birthday. This shift is happening across various strata of Christian society.

Closer to home—within my tradition—Nadia Bolz-Weber, who grew up in the very conservative Church of Christ, now serves as a Lutheran pastor who openly promotes same-sex behavior—even adding affirmations of it to the Lutheran baptismal formula. Bolz-Weber, who has become a rock star among left-wing evangelicals, goes further to suggest that viewing porn is not sinful. In the fall of 2018, she even began a campaign calling on women across America to send her the purity rings of their youth so she could melt them down and make a giant vagina idol out of them.[4]

But it is not just redefining sex that marks the rise of progressivism. In actuality, progressivism is simply a rehashing of old established themes that have marked North American theological liberalism for nearly two centuries. Rob Bell's book *Love Wins* offers a form of universalism that has been characteristic of American theological liberalism since the early 1800s.[5] Bell writes with captivating, winsome, and contemporary tones, but at the end of the day, his position can hardly be called "new." Universalism was one of the earliest doctrines of theological liberalism in America—reflected today in the Universalist Church of America. Universalism is a hallmark of old-school theological liberalism.

Popular blogger, author, and Franciscan friar Richard Rohr, with his therapeutic, self-affirming gospel, argues that the biblical doctrine of the sacrificial, atoning death of Jesus is violent and inconsistent with the actual message of Jesus.[6] He puts forth a false choice: either God loves us and we don't need atonement, or we need atonement and God doesn't love us. Rohr's readers may think that in his self-accepting message they have found a new and liberating way to conceive of Jesus. But they are actually only following a well-worn path of theological liberalism that strays from the apostolic witness. The doctrine of the atonement has been a stumbling block for liberals for two hundred years.

Take the popular figure Shane Claiborne as another example of the span of the shift. He and many others advocate that we elevate the "red letters" of the Bible over its "black letters." Claiborne believes that in the red letters of the Gospels he can find confirmation of his social theories, but he knows that he cannot find it in the black letters.[7] Claiborne and other "Red Letter Christians" may feel as though they have rediscovered the original form of the Christian faith. But their work is nothing new. The British and American deists of the 17th and 18th centuries dabbled in the exact same methodology, believing that the handful of texts that appear to confirm their theories are the key to the faith. Deist president Thomas Jefferson literally cut out many of the black letters of the New Testament—with an actual penknife—and published a red-letter volume confirming his values—a work he entitled *The Life and Morals of Jesus of Nazareth.*

Rachel Held Evans writes with a captivating and imaginative style about how to speak of the inspiration of Scripture. But ultimately she professes a view of Scripture that submits the Bible to the ever-changing sentiments of North American elites—particularly those that Evans herself holds.[8] Again, this is nothing other than old-school theological liberalism, which has gone through numerous evolutionary phases in rejecting the authority of the apostles, prophets, and witnesses of Jesus Christ. Escaping the plain teachings of Scripture is necessary for progressivism, which requires that contemporary feelings define faith rather than biblical and historic Christianity.

Lisa and Michael Gungor have packaged their newly found Christian faith in artistic and relevant-sounding ways with their *The Liturgists Podcast* (with cohost Michael McHargue), but their complete dependence upon sentiment over objective truth is nothing new.[9] As early as Ralph Waldo Emerson, theological liberals were arguing that sentiment and imagination are a superior foundation for Christian theology to the Bible, the creeds, or dogmatics. Of course by their very definition, sentiments change all the time. But this has not stopped progressives from promoting a faith built upon such shifting sand. While the "Jesus" that the Gungors and their enormously popular Liturgists initiative present doesn't look anything like the Christ of Scripture, he does look suspiciously like the Gungors themselves.

All these softer, gentler versions of theological liberalism resonate with millions of North American, upper and middle-class Christians—many of whom are desperate for a Christian faith that is consistent with the changing values of North American popular culture. For many departing evangelicals, progressivism feels new, fresh, and relevant. But it is actually not new at all—progressivism is only a replay of old-line Protestant Liberalism. This matters, because their Protestant liberalism is among the fastest dying religions *in the world*. Evangelicals are coming to liberalism at exactly the moment that liberalism is proving to provide no real life.

The Reason for the Shift

Why is this shift happening among evangelicals?

The simple answer is that evangelicals who once sought a biblical version of the Christian faith are now being lured into a form of Christianity that accommodates American secular values.

Among the highest values of secular North Americans are *inclusiveness* and *self-actualization*. And thus many Christians prefer a version of the Christian faith with open borders—universalism and permissiveness are high values for progressive Christians too. People should be affirmed no matter what they do. Anything that smacks of being judgmental is automatically dismissed. For them, historic Christianity must be redefined along the lines of secular theories of progress.

Secular North Americans prefer social action to personal responsibility, so many progressive Christians want a "Jesus" who doesn't make many *personal* demands on people but issues *policy statements* about immigration and climate change instead. The devastation caused by individual men who abandon their families for other women is of little interest to Christian progressives. But policies that force bakers to celebrate same-sex marriages are backed with ferocious rage. Abortion was once considered a grave sin by nearly every denomination. In today's North American popular culture, though, it is a "reproductive right." In order to accommodate pop culture, many Christians are now shamefully silent about abortion; large numbers have even switched sides in support of this practice, which—since the emergence of ultrasounds—is clearly the unjust taking of a human life. Many Christians are desperate to fit into the spirit of the times, so they rewrite the faith along the lines of the myth of progress.

Progressivism feels new and fresh to Christians leaving biblical Christianity behind. But in truth, progressivism is just one more version of the white, civic religion known as liberalism that has characterized elites since the early 19th century. There is hardly anything in progressive evangelicalism that hasn't been part of theological liberalism for years. It's not new to America; it's just new to evangelicals.

And it's become very attractive.

Cultural Conformity

In this book, I am challenging us to recognize the drift toward theological progressivism occurring in the lives of many disciples and even in whole churches. I want us to first see the danger progressivism poses to the gospel. In what follows, I will show that the changes progressivism makes to the Christian faith render our faith not only unbiblical and unorthodox but also ultimately un-Christian. "Progressivism" is actually just one more version of the same cultural accommodation that has plagued God's people from the very beginning. When progressive leaders alter biblical faith to accommodate American secular values, they are doing nothing new. But their actions are destructive.

Cultural conformity has always been among the greatest challenges the people of God have faced. As early as the giving of the Ten Commandments on Sinai, the Jews set out to adapt the one true God in an effort to make him more like Baal—the god of the dominant culture around them.

Have you ever wondered how cow-worship could possibly make sense to the Israelites? Well, both the Egyptians, whose land they were leaving, and the Canaanites, into whose land they were entering, worshiped cows. To get ahead in business, politics, and the neighborhood, respectable Israelites decided to just join in; when the elites accommodated cow-worship, the masses followed suit. If everybody around you is saying that a cow is a god, the social pressure on you to deify cows will be tremendous. In the same way, if everybody around you is saying that a man may be a woman, the social pressure will be enormous for you to say that men are women. It's no wonder that throughout the period of the Israelite judges and kings, idolatry and syncretism were defining problems as Jews erected altars on every tall hill and under every green tree.

In the New Testament, the church faced the same problem of conformity. Its members could sometimes see no farther than their Jewish roots; at other times, they couldn't contain their enthusiasm for Hellenistic paganism. The apostles had to fight on both sides—arguing, on one hand, that we are not justified by being faithful Jews, and on the other hand, that Christians must not act like the pagans around them.

History tells us that in the four hundred-year gap between the Old and New Testaments, accommodating to the surrounding culture was a constant challenge for Jews. Many Jews blindly assumed Greek culture—even taking Greek names for their children. At times, Hellenism was forced upon the Jews, but convincing the Jews to adapt didn't take much effort. Modern archaeologists are continually finding ancient Jewish synagogues with pagan signs of the zodiac depicted in lovely mosaic floors.

And every Christian denomination today has its own form of accommodation to the culture that produced it—sometimes subtle, other times overt.

The greatest challenge of syncretism for North American churches today is the challenge of progressivism. For years, progressivism was largely confined to mainline liberal denominations and a handful of universities. But in the last thirty years, progressivism has become a major challenge for people and institutions who were once solidly committed to apostolic Christianity. In Europe, liberalism lived a short life before most Europeans became functionally unbelieving. In North America, liberalism has survived nearly two hundred years, although in most of its institutional forms it is currently on life-support.

Ironically, as mainline liberal denominations in America are breathing their last breaths, many evangelicals and Bible-believing Christians are taking up the exact same tenets of dying progressivism. Many pulpits, colleges, blogs, and books—in addition to popular speakers in Baptist churches, Independent Christian churches, some Community churches, Wesleyan churches, a cappella churches of Christ, and other evangelical churches—are currently making fateful decisions that will determine their destiny. Will they choose the apostolic faith handed down through the millennia, or will they continually redefine the faith to fit into America's increasingly pagan culture? The battle is growing, and a positive outcome is critical for the health of future generations of Christians.

A Renewal of Apostolic Christianity

And I believe there is hope!

While progressivism today is challenging the source of authority for Christianity, its ultimate meaning, and, of course, the nature of its founder, Jesus Christ, the discussion is not closed. American Christians are currently debating progressivism and questioning its credence. We still have time to renew our commitment to the lordship of King Jesus, the apostolic witness of Scripture, and the disciple-making mission of the church.

Theology lies along a spectrum, which includes progressivism. I know people are at various places on the spectrum. Some of you who are reading this book are disillusioned evangelicals—typically, millennials who have been hurt by or turned off by the misadventures of biblical Christians, or who are attracted to progressive social action. Some of you are solidly evangelical—pastors, ministers, elders, or laypersons—who have been hearing messages from your pulpit, from books or blogs, or from Christian schools that seem to challenge the Scriptures and historic Christian faith. Others of you are deliberate and thought-out progressives, who are blazing a new path for the Christian faith—one that reinterprets the ancient faith in light of Western values.

Whatever your current position, I welcome you to this book, which constitutes a call for renewal. The book is written in conjunction with Renew—an international group of like-minded pastors, scholars, professionals, and laypersons who are passionate about reclaiming the foundations of biblical Christianity and the mission of disciple making in the name of King Jesus for the 21st-century church.

Let me state clearly my goal. I want to provoke a renewal of the apostolic faith Jesus gave the apostles and instructed them to give to the whole world. I take my cue from Ephesians 2:13-22:

> So then you are no longer strangers and aliens, but you
> are fellow citizens with the saints and members of the
> household of God, *built on the foundation of the apostles
> and prophets, Christ Jesus himself being the cornerstone*, in
> whom the whole structure, being joined together, grows
> into a holy temple in the Lord. In him you also are being
> built together into a dwelling place for God by the Spirit.

In this text, Paul affirms that the people of God are to be a holy temple—even in the middle of an unholy world. Paul affirms that in Christ, we are no longer strangers to one another or to God but are fellow citizens in God's family. And, Paul affirms, we access Jesus *through the work of the holy apostles and prophets.*

In short, I want to provoke a renewal of the faith that Jesus entrusted to the apostles and prophets, which has now been bequeathed to us in the sacred Scriptures. It is this faith that progressivism challenges. My hope is that you'll see the clear choice you must make when you declare yourself a follower of Jesus in North America.

I say "North America" because theological progressivism is largely a North American phenomenon—that is, it's largely a religion of the one percent. Most Western Europeans have given up on theological liberalism and opted for a general disregard of Christianity altogether. Few believers in the global South and in Latin America would ever dream of being theologically progressive. They have too much respect for the sacred treasure of the Scriptures. Indeed, even in North America, progressivism is typically not the religion of those coming to faith in Jesus but rather the religion of those who are restlessly seeking an alternative to their faith. Most people become theologically progressive only after giving up on orthodoxy. Progressive authors and speakers such as Jen Hatmaker are less popular among *unbelievers*—even if celebrities and unbelievers applaud them. Instead, progressive Christians are typically most popular among *evangelicals who want a Christianity that fits America's secular values.* Such authors and speakers are popular among those who are leaving biblical Christianity behind.

This means that progressivism often consists of the following:

- A rewrite of historic Christianity to accommodate those who want some version of religion and ethics in their lives but who prefer American sensibilities to historic Christianity;
- An unnatural way of reading Scripture to make it fit into the prevailing values of the Anglo West;
- A less-than-forthright use of the great Christian creeds, where the same words might be said but new North American meanings are applied;
- A rereading of Christian history that often understates the great stream of orthodoxy and focuses, instead, on minor Christian streams in support of American progressive particularities.

So, as I said, theological progressivism is largely a North American enterprise. Ask for orthodox historic forms of Christianity in Latin America, and hundreds of millions of people will raise their hands. Drop a Bible into Africa, and millions of orthodox Christians spring up. The same is true for China, India, Southeast Asia, and Eastern Europe. I've traveled to many of these places and seen it with my own eyes. Indeed, there is no place on earth where non-believers would read a Bible and naturally think to become a theological progressive.

This is true even for ordinary non-Christian Americans and it accounts for the dearth of conversions liberal churches experience. Once the Christian faith is stripped of the distinctives taught by the apostles and prophets, who were actually entrusted by Jesus to define the Christian faith, why would anyone really want to waste their time on it? What is left that would attract unbelievers to faith if everybody is pretty much already "okay," if the Bible isn't to be trusted in its plain teachings, and if the primary interest of the Christian faith is mere public policy? Why would an ordinary, unbelieving American want to leave disbelief for Christian progressivism? As we will see below, progressivism is a religion typically driven by the idea that we humans can and should build a social utopia here in this life. But if we can build this utopia by ourselves, why bother with Jesus?[10]

So theological liberalism is not an on-ramp to the Christian faith; it is an off-ramp. And, as the past one hundred and fifty years of liberalism have shown, it is an off-ramp with few guardrails.

Lesslie Newbigin was a British theologian who spent years serving as a missionary in India. When he returned to his native England late in life, he was dismayed at how unbelieving England had become and how much British Christianity had given up on historic, orthodox, and biblical theology for theological progressivism. He argued that England and the West had not left *faith* altogether to become godless; rather, he pointed out, England and much of British Christianity had become pagan in order to serve *false gods*. Saddened by theological progressivism, Newbigin called for a renewed commitment to orthodox Christianity—a new conversion: a conversion back to apostolic Christianity in our era. Such a paradigm shift will lead to a "new vision of how things are and, not at once but gradually, to the development of a new possibility structure in which the most real of all realities is the living God whose character is rendered for us in the pages of Scripture."[11]

In this same vein, I invite you to read this call to renew historic, orthodox, and biblical Christianity as an urgent appeal to embrace the faith "once and for all delivered," as the brother of Jesus put it (Jude 1:3).[12] For some of you, this will mean rethinking the entire myth of progress with its utopian view of self-defining autonomy—a myth dearly embraced by Americans. For others, it will require you to set aside the need to be relevant and cool. For many of us, it will take overcoming spiritual cowardice and sloth to step up to true freedom—the freedom to look the power brokers of America straight in the eye and say, "No." Choose the sacred trust handed to you from Christ himself, through the holy apostles, the martyrs and doctors of the church, the great creeds, and the sacred Scriptures. Choose the real thing. Choose the truth and beauty of biblical faith.

I'm sure that Jen Hatmaker, our key example of progressivism here, is a warm and likeable person. But I believe her positions have become dangerous for the Christian faith, even though I didn't always think this. Hatmaker once made a statement that I think summarizes my book. I'll let her define the danger that progressive Christianity poses: "We've invented a thousand shades of gray, devising a comfortable Christian existence we can all live with—super awesome, except the Bible doesn't support it."[13] That is the point at issue.

Chapter 1
A Clear Choice

When I was twenty-five years old, I was accepted into the New Testament Ph.D. program at Vanderbilt's Graduate Department of Religion. I was thrilled but also a bit nervous—only four of us were accepted into the program. I felt the pressure.

The students before me and behind me hailed from such universities as Princeton, Johns Hopkins, Union, Columbia, Yale, and the like. Not me. I had attended a small denominational school in rural Tennessee of which no one had ever heard. I was from a conservative fellowship where it was not uncommon to frown upon graduate work in religion. Because I was one of the only two or three "biblical Christians" I knew in the entire Graduate Department of Religion (GDR), I figured my love for orthodox Christianity would be challenged. Looking back, I realize that I was willing to take the risk of losing my faith to get the degree.

At Vanderbilt, as one might expect, I experienced radical liberalism. Biblical Christianity was considered the enemy, and pretty much every leftist social theory was entertained. Back then, deconstructionism, radical feminist hermeneutics, and liberation theology were all the rage. We read the works of postmodern authors like Levi-Strauss, Foucault, and Derrida. And everybody seemed to agree that much of Christianity was a power play on the part of upper class, white heterosexual males to control the rest of the world—something I still find odd, given that the majority of students in the GDR were upper class, white heterosexual males.

At first, I tried to listen to progressivism with a warm ear. Some of the objections against biblical and orthodox Christianity were fair, and I tried to be honest about that. But much of what I saw was fueled more by anger than by reason. There were protests, rage-filled students writing angry papers, political rallies, and a variety of attempts to tear down social structures that had taken generations to build.

I began to see the plasticity of progressivism in the fact that it seemed to change its dance every time secularism changed its tune. In the 1970s, many progressives had wistfully admired Pol Pot and the utopia he promised—even though there was evidence early on of a massive holocaust in Cambodia. A decade later, when I was at Vanderbilt, the evidence of genocide had forced these same progressives to "unlike" him, although some of those in the religion program could never quite condemn him. I remember students and faculty opposed Bill Clinton when, as a presidential candidate from the state of Arkansas, his infidelities and alleged sexual assaults were revealed. But when he won the nomination, they dismissed (or even blamed) his "bimbo" accusers and fully supported him. They hated censorship, until they wrote guidelines banning certain language from the university's religion programs. In each case, progressive Christianity seemed desperate to appear to be on the "right side of history"—even when the right side of history was wrong.

Beyond Vanderbilt, progressive religion appeared to have no limits in its willingness to shock. There were condom distributions, a homoerotic Jesus, resolutions in support of Lenin (who had been dead for more than sixty years at that point), bans on calling God "Father" and in his place worshiping the "mother earth goddess," financial support of the Sandinistas, etc. The liberalism I saw in Vanderbilt's religion program seemed permanently stuck in the radicalism of the '60s.[14]

By the end of my second year at Vandy, I was thoroughly disillusioned with progressivism. It seemed to me inconsistent with its own claims, destructive, and deeply cynical. I found most of its challenges to the Bible unfounded, and many of its theories about early Christianity just speculations built on guesses. Those who questioned the Bible mostly seemed to be angry that the text wouldn't confirm their desires and passions.

By the time I had finished my dissertation and graduated, I had become more convinced than ever that the Bible is a beautiful, true, and honest gift from God and that it deserves our obedience. At Vanderbilt, I fell deeply in love with the Bible and biblical Christianity. Instead of leaning into progressivism, I turned against it. I didn't learn to dislike progressivism by listening to someone like the politically conservative talk show host Rush Limbaugh. (I *don't* listen to him.) Instead, I learned to dislike progressivism by studying the Bible—among progressives. Working closely with and befriending progressives during my time at Vanderbilt revealed to me the error of their ways. I'm sharing my experience with you so that you too may see the error of their ways because I think their ways are not only misguided *but also harmful.*

One event in particular while at Vanderbilt represents how these experiences shaped my thinking about progressivism. Vanderbilt had invited author and scholar C. K. Barrett to speak at one of our annual lectureships. As part of his visit, the New Testament Ph.D. students and faculty were invited to a lunch with him, one of the highlights of my time at Vanderbilt. C. K. Barrett was a professor of divinity at the University of Durham (England), a prolific author, and a brilliant New Testament thinker—one of the greatest English-speaking New Testament scholars of the 20th century. We had all read his works.

Students asked lots of questions at lunch, and Barrett responded with brilliance, scholarship, and gentleness. One question came up about gender. A student didn't like what the Bible says about sex and gender and asked Professor Barrett how to develop a biblical theology that fits contemporary sex and gender interests.

"You cannot legitimately dismiss what the Bible says about sex and gender," Barrett responded. "Not if you want to be honest. It says what it says. The only question is whether or not you believe it."

Even though it wasn't my question in the first place, I wanted to push a little further, so I asked the professor a follow-up question: "What if I just cannot accept what the Bible says?" I asked it as a hypothetical, but this scholar of the New Testament took it as a challenge. The only time he seemed agitated the whole day was when I asked my question.

His face a bit flushed, Barrett put down his drink, looked me in the eyes, and sternly said in his thick British accent, "Then, you need to find another religion. The Christian religion isn't open for negotiation."

Is the Christian religion open for negotiation? Jesus, the apostles, and the prophets didn't think so, which is why they laid down the foundations of the faith, as Jude says, "once and for all." But progressivism isn't so sure.

What is Theological Progressivism?[15]

As I studied the Scriptures at Vanderbilt, I discovered their great truth, honesty, and power. I learned to deconstruct them, as Ph.D. students are taught to do, but I was also able to put them back together afterwards—to find an amazing book that still changes lives. My postgraduate minor was in early Christian history, and I fell in love with orthodoxy, listening to the great masters of our faith. I had previous academic work in history, and I knew that many, if not most, of the greatest humanitarian accomplishments in the West were the product of apostolic Christianity. So by the time I left Vanderbilt, I was profoundly in love with Christian orthodoxy and the Bible from which it sprang. I finished my Ph.D. in Religious Studies with a higher view of Scripture and the belief that the Christian faith is not negotiable. But not every Ph.D. student does so. Consider the path of Pete Enns for whom the Christian faith *is* negotiable.

Pete Enns has a different view of apostolic faith. Enns, born only a few days after I was, is a favorite author for many progressives. He began his career as a religion professor at Westminster Seminary, having received his Ph.D. in the Ancient Near East from Harvard University. He has worked in several important areas of religion, including with the BioLogos Foundation, an organization connected to Francis Collins, director of the National Institutes of Health. BioLogos seeks to demonstrate the compatibility of faith with science.

During his time at Westminster, however, Enns began to say things about the Bible that unsettled some of his constituency. Enns published some of these opinions in his widely read book *Inspiration and Incarnation*. Though Enns argued for the inspiration of the Bible, he also emphasized the human dimension of the Scriptures—enough so that the board of Princeton eventually terminated his job. After this painful time, Enns began to move in a direction opposite mine.

Since leaving Westminster, Enns has increasingly departed from apostolic Christianity—openly negotiating with the historic faith in order to produce a faith more compatible with secular Western values. His 2014 work, *The Bible Tells Me So*, argues against the historicity of large portions of the Bible. It suggests that much of the image of God presented in the Old Testament is not only wrong but also diabolical. And the book insists that the Bible does not give us a consistent ethical system, and so it seems the best we can hope for is a Bible that journeys with us while we sort out our own ethical values. In all of this, Enns appeals to "scholarship" and "history," but beneath such appeals really lies the conviction that we must negotiate the faith in order to make it compatible with contemporary Western elitist sensibilities.

This is, ultimately, the heart of progressivism: we must always be moving beyond what the apostles and orthodox Christianity have bequeathed to us in order to make a Christian faith that suits our contemporary sensibilities. In this sense, even *evangelical* progressivism is nothing other than full-blown theological liberalism waiting to happen. If liberalism is racing toward the cliff at a hundred miles per hour, evangelical progressivism is racing toward the same destination, only at seventy-five miles per hour.

Assessing the Tenets of Progressivism

And so, before we go any farther, let's get a handle on what theological liberalism is and how it developed. Some will be surprised to know that theological liberalism, with its broader vision of progressivism, is a relatively modern phenomenon, as I mentioned in brief above, and that it has fairly well-established canons. Indeed, some will be surprised to learn that progressivism is a peculiar historical movement, and not, as some seem to think, "just the way things are." By going over the history of progressivism, including its most liberal forms, we will better understand what progressivism is, whence it came, and where it is going.

North American liberal progressivism sprang from a 19th century movement developed by aristocratic white pastors, poets, and academicians for the purpose of creating a civic religion that promoted Victorian virtues for the newly-formed republic of the United States.[16]

To be accessible to a broad range of white citizens, theological liberalism required Jesus to be more of an ethicist than the Son of God. It also required that reason and experience be given priority over divine revelation and Christian doctrine. Religious sentiment, social action, and political concerns soon eclipsed personal holiness and salvation from sin to become the defining concerns of the Christian faith. Progressivism became a religion all its own.

For theological progressives, humans were no longer regarded as corrupt and inherently sinful like they had been by the Calvinists before them. Rather, humans—especially the white, urban, and educated ones—were optimistically regarded as partly divine and fully capable of constructing their own republican paradise here on the North American continent. As a result of the demands of progressivism, many core orthodoxies of the Christian faith had to be redefined, downplayed, or even eliminated. Let's look at some of the most critical ones.

Jesus' divinity. One of the first orthodoxies to fall was the fundamental Christian claim that Jesus is the divine Son of God. Unitarianism—the earliest institutional form of progressivism—required that Jesus be redefined from Son of God to mere role model for social reform. Because progressives believe that humans are inherently good, the cross is not needed and Jesus doesn't have to be "God incarnate." Instead, for progressives Jesus is simply a role model for living an ethical and just life. From this assumption it follows, then, that the doctrine of the atoning death of Jesus is no longer comprehensible—if everybody's okay, we don't need to be rescued from sin. Many progressives find the Bible's teachings on atonement utterly reprehensible. One of the hallmarks of today's evangelical progressivism is a tendency to focus only on the human work of Jesus "the activist" or "the ethicist," downplaying his divinity, if not totally denying it.

Scripture as final authority. Progressives regarded the doctrine of the authority of Scripture as standing in the way of sensibility, experience, and reason, so Scripture had to be devalued. At first, Scripture was turned into poetry, but in the closing years of the 19th century, it was subjected to acidic evaluations by American academicians who were glad to discover that German universities had deconstructed the Scriptures half a century earlier. Biblical claims of miracles, such as the virgin birth and the resurrection, were considered hopelessly linked to the prescientific worldviews of antiquity. Often, they were treated as quaint metaphors; at other times, they were simply dismissed. Evangelical progressives today accept the assumptions of old-line historic liberalism, namely, something cannot be true if we don't feel that it's true. So no authority—including the Bible—can be right if it contradicts our sensibilities. This explains why progressives continue publishing reinterpretations of the Bible.

Darwin and the Bible. Darwinism, which hit the English-speaking world like a meteor, forced liberals to reconsider how they read the Bible. The creation account of Scripture could no longer be taken historically, and perhaps the entire Bible was more mythical than historical. Mythical, poetic, and even dismissive hermeneutics were developed by progressives for the purpose of updating biblical theology to bring it into line with the work of Darwin and other scientific enterprises for progressive purposes. Many progressives exaggerated the differences between contemporary science and the biblical narrative. But such exaggerations actually demonstrate something of a bias among progressives. African Americans believe in science as much as white elites, but they are much more likely to believe that the Bible is the actual Word of God than general Protestants. Exaggerating the distance between the modern sciences and the Bible belittles the viewpoints of many African American Christians.[17]

Progress and human nature. Biased toward the white Anglo-Saxon race, a number of progressives worked toward racial purity through *eugenics*, which was a liberal enterprise based on the conviction that white, English-speaking people are destined to civilize the whole world.[18] Eugenics sprang from an attempt to cleanse the human race of inferiors along the lines of Darwin's natural selection. Eugenics was not a conservative enterprise; it was a progressive one based on the belief that humanity can only achieve true progress if undesirables are prevented from reproducing. Even those liberals who did not advocate for eugenics found themselves having to reconsider the entire framework of anthropology—now believing that we humans are not the work of a creator God but rather of blind chance. The ability among progressives to adapt the Christian faith to the precepts of Darwin signaled refinement and sophistication. Progressives considered anyone who rejected Darwinianism as anti-scientific, backward, and fundamentalist. Evangelical progressives today pay homage to science—often opening sentences with the loose phrase "the science says." But progressives are often the least scientific of Christians, as they tend to be blinded from simple facts by a utopian ideology. For example, there is no *scientific* question about when human life begins; it begins at conception. But there is an *ideological* question, and evangelical progressives tend to shut their eyes to *science* for the sake of *ideology* when the disgrace of abortion comes up. No blindness is as dark as the willful blindness of ideology.

The authority of the church. In the face of the democratic and empirical spirit of North American progressives, the authority of creeds and ecclesiastical structures hardly stood a chance. Rather, theories of science, social theory, and political advocacy became authorities for progressives. Downplaying the orthodox doctrine of the second coming of Christ, progressives began to interpret Christian eschatology with a post-millennial mindset—coming to believe that the very work that progressives were doing constituted the thousand-year reign of Christ mentioned in Revelation 20. In this view, progressives themselves are the coming messiahs. This eschatological view of progressivism fueled America's political sense of Manifest Destiny: white Anglo-Saxon Protestant virtues are destined to conquer the continent and eventually the farthest corners of the globe as progressives build the kingdom of God here on earth.

Evangelical progressives today continue this heritage, largely ignoring personal sin and insisting, instead, upon political theories—sometimes with good results but often at the cost of neglecting the destructive bondage sin levels upon individual people. Systems may be broken, but they are broken because individuals are broken. Progressivism largely ignores this fundamental truth because insisting on personal accountability requires serious personal change on the part of individuals, and it feels judgmental. Advocating for social change requires very little personal change, but it *feels* very ethical.

Public policy as the gospel. By adapting, liberal progressivism in the 20th century survived two world wars, the Great Depression, and the Cold War. Early on, progressives took on social causes such as prostitution, alcoholism, women's suffrage, workers' rights, and poverty, among others. Already a civic religion, progressivism depended heavily upon the government and other public institutions to achieve its goals. Massive reform movements and progressive projects joined forces with government to achieve what was perceived as a more just society, characterized by the 19th amendment, the passage and then repeal of prohibition, eugenics, labor reforms, the Civil Rights Movement, anti-war protests, abortion, gay rights, and the like. All were inspired by liberal progressivism's desire to create a virtuous nation through public policy and civic religion.

One should applaud much of the social action of liberalism in the 20th century, as it provided correctives to a number of grave injustices—especially civil rights for women and African Americans. Indeed, it is only fair to point out that liberalism was, in the 20th century, sometimes more closely aligned with biblical Christianity than were biblical Christians themselves. But as with other movements, progressivism has overplayed its hand in the area of public policy, and often its issues are extreme and its proposals misguided or even harmful.

A bend toward Marxism. Already suspicious of industrialism and capitalism, 19th-century liberals flirted with Marxism in the early and mid-20th century. Some theological liberals went as far as to fully embrace Marxism—in spite of Marx's hostility toward religion. Such movements as liberation theology became popular among various theologians in Latin America and within North American universities. Most progressives did not become outright Marxists, but almost all progressives have fully adopted Marx's view of history as warfare between the social classes. Class warfare as identity politics has in fact become a defining characteristic of contemporary theological liberalism—dividing humanity into various social groups, then pitting them against each other in a supposed struggle for justice: blacks against whites, women against men, gays against straights, immigrants against citizens. Consistent with Marxist impulses, theological progressives always pick the side they perceive to be the underdog, relentlessly attacking its enemies and insisting that one must only "punch up" and never down. This explains why theological liberalism cannot bring itself to criticize various groups even when such groups exhibit very bad behavior. This also explains why progressivism is always searching for a new class of privileged people to topple—exempting only itself.[19]

Salvation as self-actualization. In the last half-century, theological progressivism has begun adapting American psychology to bolster its agenda. Since the highest personal good in much of American psychology is self-actualization, liberal progressivism seeks to aid people in the pursuit of self-acceptance and authenticity. The highest individual virtue among theological progressives is discovering who you feel you are and then having your feelings affirmed by those around you. Progressives are constantly changing to keep up with the latest experiences people have. It's considered a sign of virtue among progressives to leave the door open for the next change (hence the *plus* sign in "LGBTQ+").

The sexual revolution. In the 1960s, the baby boomer generation started coming of age. A rebellious and self-indulgent generation, progressive baby boomers created the sexual revolution, turning generations of sexual ethics upside down. It had taken centuries for Westerners to create a just and loving system for managing human sexual appetites through the institution of Christian marriage, which teaches men that they cannot indulge their every sexual urge. In Christian marriage, men must commit themselves to one woman for life and offer their body to their wife in an act of mutual honor and devotion.

The sexual revolution, fueled by both the birth control pill and the hippy ethic, taught both men and women that sex is merely a matter of pleasure, no commitment or love required. The damage done by progressivism's sexual revolution is the greatest social injustice of our time—millions of lives have been permanently damaged by the sexual ethic of the left, as millions have been born and abandoned by parents moving on to new sexual and relational adventures. And this does not include the millions of lives cut short in the abhorrent practice of abortion. One cannot be sure where the next change in sexual ethics among progressives will lead, but even such practices as pederasty are now being given a hearing among those on the far left.

Commandeering universities and denominations. As early as the late 18th century, liberalism was taking over American universities—virtually all of which started out as orthodox Christian schools.[20] Like a long string of divorces, various reformers reacted to these liberal takeovers by founding new schools, only to discover their own schools had fallen under the spell of progressivism—from Harvard, to Yale, to Princeton, to Westminster, just to name a few.

By the middle and late 20th century, liberal progressivism had taken over not only many universities but also the leadership of most mainline Protestant denominations. Episcopalians, Lutherans, Reformed churches, Presbyterians, the Disciples of Christ, Methodists, and even some Baptists found themselves bitterly divided between orthodox and progressive members and leaders. Most denominations split; some have split several times.

Progressives consider orthodox members a nuisance; orthodox members consider progressives heretics.

Moving into evangelicalism. In the last twenty years or so, many evangelicals—who were once solid counterweights to theological progressivism—have begun to flirt with progressivism. Especially among millennials, orthodoxy, biblical authority, and historic Christianity are increasingly seen as the enemies of what they call "social justice," "inclusiveness," and "the kingdom of God." For evangelical progressives, or more precisely progressives who were formerly evangelical, the work of the Christian faith is largely one of social reform and public policy.

Thus, though many progressive evangelicals still identify with non-liberal denominations, they do allow progressive theology to tell them which questions to ask (such as gender, sexual orientation, climate and economic justice, and immigration). For example, many evangelical bloggers and writers seem to write endlessly about how to accommodate progressive values about sexual orientation, rather than, say, describe how Christ can set us free from sexual bondage. And increasingly, many evangelicals are turning to theological liberals for their answers. In fact, there is a growing movement among evangelical leaders, Christian schools, and many churches away from the apostolic witness of Scripture and toward a mildly religious version of left-leaning, American secularism.

The theological justification for progressive evangelicalism is often rooted in a particular interpretation of Scripture that identifies the term "kingdom of God" in the Synoptics with contemporary progressive social action.[21] While the gospel absolutely includes social concerns such as justice and mercy in this life, at its heart the gospel is about Christ's atoning sacrifice, his coronation as king, and his future return to establish a new heaven and earth. Defining the kingdom of God as socialism, or even as mere social reform, is problematic on numerous levels:

- It forces modern social interests onto an ancient Jewish and Christian concept;
- It deliberately ignores Paul's writings, which are our earliest written witness to Jesus;

- It downplays the fourth Gospel's near-complete lack of interest in the term (preferring to emphasize the fullness of "life" and the divinity of Jesus instead);
- It pretends that some of the red letters of the Gospels are superior to the Bible's black letters;[22]
- It subordinates the rest of the witness of the apostles and prophets (James, Peter, Jude, and John) to contemporary sensibilities—or simply dismisses their witness altogether.

While all these stand against orthodox Christian faith, the greatest challenge presented by the current trend to read "kingdom of God" as "progressive social action" is its modulation, or even denial, of personal sin and the personal need for salvation. Social structures need saving, yes. But individuals also need saving, and increased funding for a particular government program will not save the eternal lives of individual sinners. Only personal faith in Christ can do this, but progressivism is not interested in that. Conflating the kingdom of God with contemporary social justice theory results in our denying such biblical doctrines as personal faith in and obedience to Jesus. It is simply a fact that social justice theories often let individuals off the hook for individual sins. So long as someone tweets the right cause, votes to the left, and signals the latest approved policy or social position, their personal life—no matter how bad—is given a pass. It's worth remembering that the brother of Jesus declares true religion to be "caring for the widow and orphan," *as well as* "keeping oneself unstained from the world" (Jam. 1:27).

This tendency to reinterpret the gospel of Christ as a social program loosely identified with the "kingdom of God" represents a radical turn from biblical and orthodox Christianity. In Scripture and orthodox Christianity, the starting point of the gospel is the recognition that humans cannot save themselves—not through obedience to the Torah and not through social action. According to the Word of God, only God can build the kingdom. We don't build it, and if we try to do so, we will end up with another kingdom—either our own or somebody else's.

Further, in Scripture (including the red-letter sections) only personal faith in Christ can save a person. Thus, though both individuals and people groups are lost, the only way to save humanity is through personal faith in Christ, personal repentance, and personal holiness. When individuals turn from their sin and respond to Jesus in obedient faith, justice and mercy will result. When elites seek to affect social change apart from individual repentance and discipleship, it often results in unjust and unmerciful conduct—ranging from indulgence to coercion, or even to persecution. The divide between those who believe in the gospel of personal salvation from sin and those who believe in collectivist salvation through social action is growing, and the latter always veers into full-fledged liberalism before completely exiting the bus at general unbelief.

All this leaves us in early 21st-century America with two major camps of Christian theology and practice: on one side is orthodox, biblical Christianity, which includes evangelicals, many ethnic churches, and conservative Catholics. On the other side is progressive Christianity, which includes many mainline Protestants, coastal aristocrats, and disillusioned evangelicals.

So what do progressives believe? Liberal theologian Scotty McLennan sums it up:

> The Bible is meant to be read largely metaphorically and allegorically, rather than literally. Science and religion are compatible; we are committed to the use of logic, reason, and the scientific method. Doubt is a handmaiden of faith. Love is a primary Christian value, and it is directly related to the promotion of liberty and justice in society at large. All people are inherently equal and worthy of dignity and respect. Free religious expression should be governmentally protected, but no particular tradition should be established as the state religion. There are many roads to the top of the spiritual mountain, and Christianity is only one of them. Interfaith understanding and tolerance are critical. We see Jesus primarily as a spiritual and ethical teacher and less as being identical with God. Living a fulfilled and ethical life here and now is more important than speculating on what happens to us after we die. Non-violence is strongly preferred in relationships between human beings, groups, and nations. Women and men must play an equal role in

religious leadership. And in terms of current American
hot-button issues, we tend to be pro-choice on abortion
and in favor of marriages for same-sex couples.[23]

McClennan succinctly sums up what *committed* progressives believe,
but *run-of-the-mill* progressivism is much less interesting than this. Progressivism is, in the end, about humans, not about God. And so, progressive religion often boils down to a sort of therapeutic deism. As Dreher
says, most non-biblical Americans—including progressives—have five basic religious tenets: 1) a God exists who created and ordered the world and
watches over human life on earth; 2) God wants people to be good, nice,
and fair to each other as taught in the Bible and by most world religions;
3) the central goal of life is to be happy and feel good about oneself; 4)
God doesn't need to be particularly involved in our lives except when he's
needed to resolve a problem; and 5) all good people die and go to heaven.[24]

How widespread is theological progressivism? From the seat of a typical American evangelical, it might appear that progressivism is taking over
the world. In fact, however, the opposite is true. As already noted, where
the Christian faith is currently exploding—across the Global South, for
example—progressivism is almost never mentioned. Further, the official
position of the vast majority of established Christian churches is very *unprogressive*—founded upon the divinity of Jesus, convicted by his atoning
death, proclaiming his coming judgment, believing in the authority of the
Scriptures, calling for personal holiness, and so on. These churches include the 1.2 billion Roman Catholics, the quarter of a billion Orthodox
Church members, the two hundred million Baptists, the tens of millions
of Pentecostals, the millions of conservative, non-Western Anglicans and
Methodists, Bible churches, most Community churches, and many other
fellowships and denominations. If you compared membership in liberal
denominations to that of orthodox and biblical denominations, liberalism
might account for less than five percent of worldwide Christianity. More
than 95 percent of the world's Christians belong to churches that teach historic, orthodox Christianity. Progressive theology is actually the religion of
the declining few.[25]

The reason progressivism has such enormous influence in America is
that it has control over several historically important denominations, and

it has formed powerful alliances with non-theological liberal institutions that possess enormous influence—including left-leaning political interests, left-leaning educational institutions, the media and entertainment industries, and a thousand other left-leaning organizations. Many of these institutions are truly godless and secular to the core; some are openly hostile toward Christian values. But that has not stopped theological progressives from finding common cause with them. This alliance makes it seem as though the whole world is becoming theologically progressive and that only a few backward conservatives remain, when the opposite is actually true. I think one day theological liberalism will be only a blip on the radar of Christian history. Progressivism is one more ideology founded upon the North American myth of progress, which has no staying power. There will come a time when progressivism is no more and biblical Christianity stands firm forever.

Ironically, Pete Enns, while trying to undermine biblical Christianity, actually makes the case for submitting to the apostolic witness. He explains: "Reading the Bible responsibly and respectfully today means learning what it meant for ancient Israelites to talk about God the way they did, and not pushing alien expectations onto texts written long ago and far away."[26] Of course, Enns believes that Bible-believing Christians are misreading the Scriptures. But nobody plays as loose with the Sacred Scriptures as do progressives. Enns is right: we must respect the Scriptures enough to learn what they mean. Apostolic Christianity goes further: we must respect the Scriptures enough *to do what they say.*

Because these things are true, we owe it to ourselves to test the assumptions of progressivism. An honest assessment will make it clear that theological progressivism is actually something of a "halfway house" for those leaving the Christian faith for unbelief altogether. It's where you go when you're giving up on the lordship of Jesus, the reality of sin and evil, the authority of revelation, the personal call to holiness, and the future blessedness of a new creation—but you still want some form of religion. Progressivism is the last step one takes before leaving the Christian faith altogether. Think of it as a "gateway drug."

So, with progressivism pressing in hard upon the Christian faith in America, we must educate ourselves as to its signs and dangers. We'll begin in the next chapter by looking at an important blog post written by a wise woman who saw from the front seat a biblical church drift into theological progressivism.

Chapter 2
Signs of Progressivism

Not long ago, Alisa Childers wrote a blog post that has since been widely read called "5 Signs Your Church Might be Heading Toward Progressive Christianity" (www.alisachilders.com). In the article, she describes her experience at a popular evangelical church that gradually embraced progressive Christianity. Before attending that church, she had never heard much about progressivism. But over time, Childers and her husband began to hear things that simply didn't align with the Bible nor with what she knew to be historic, orthodox Christianity. Eventually, the couple left that church, dismayed at what it had become.

I want to thank Childers for the clarity and honesty of her article. Since she says what I want to say better than I can, I want to use her thoughts and words and present her material for you to see where progressivism stands and where it can lead if not corrected. Childers explains that churches and pastors signal their lean toward progressivism through certain cues:

1. A lower view of the Bible

Childers points out that she began to perceive a lower view of the Bible among some of the leaders of her church. Historically, Christians have viewed the Bible as the ultimate authority for following Jesus—as the very Word of God that determines what we should believe and how we should live (I argue this point extensively in chapters below). Instead of such a high view of the Bible, in churches that are becoming progressive, you might hear subtle comments such as:

- "The Bible is a human book."
- "The apostle Paul was wrong about that."
- "The biblical authors simply didn't understand sexuality as we do."
- "The Bible merely contains the Word of God (as opposed to the Bible *is the Word of God*)."

Each of these statements reflects the belief that *our* thoughts and feelings reign over the Scriptures, and that only in areas where Scripture supports what we're saying do we deem it credible and authoritative.

2. Feelings over facts

As the Bible ceases to be viewed as God's definitive Word in progressive churches, a person's feelings become the ultimate authority for faith and practice. Honestly, that's to be expected in a North American world saturated with reality television, talk shows that emphasize people who are "true to themselves," and the value of feeling authentic. In churches that are becoming progressive, you might hear such things as:

- "That Scripture verse just doesn't resonate with me."
- "I thought homosexuality was a sin until I met and befriended some gay people."
- "Jesus just wouldn't send people to hell."

Behind each of these types of comments lies the conviction that something can only be true if I *feel* it is true. And, of course, such a methodology is self-authenticating because once a person defines the Christian faith to be whatever they *feel*, then as they adapt the apostolic faith to their feelings, they will … well, feel good.

Allow me to note, however, that most of the progressives I know have deeper levels of feelings that indicate they actually know they've done damage to Christianity or their own faith or both. This explains why progressivism can often manifest as cynicism and anger—progressives are often forced to live with the dissonance that results from their feelings, which never really line up with reality. Many progressives don't actually feel that good.

It also explains why many progressives eventually abandon Christianity altogether. Gilding biblical truths with mere feelings is only a short-term fix; in my experience, many progressives eventually realize that they cannot continue to hold both the Bible and their feelings. Tragically, they abandon Christianity altogether. It's sad to say this, but I've seen progressives who over a long period of time have become completely uninterested in Christianity. I can't help but think this will also play out in their children's lives. This is why I say that progressivism is actually only a halfway house on the way out of the faith altogether.

3. Essential Christian doctrines open for reinterpretation

Childers quotes progressive author John Pavlovitz on this point: "There are no sacred cows [in Progressive Christianity] .... Tradition, dogma, and doctrine are all fair game, because all pass through the hands of flawed humanity." Progressives must wrestle against historic Christianity in order to retain their faith. The most liberal progressives sometimes just say that biblical truths are wrong and they keep moving. But progressive pastors, authors, professors, and bloggers more frequently try to reinterpret Christian doctrines to make them palatable to the sensibilities of contemporary Westerners.

Of course, involved in this redefining of biblical terms is the art and science of hermeneutics. Progressives are regularly updating their hermeneutics in order to adapt Scripture to their sensibilities. We must go there with them, look at what the text says (not how it makes people feel), and engage such progressives using established hermeneutical principles like author's intended meaning, original context, and the meaning of words. Of course, one can fall off the other side of the boat and get sidetracked in fruitless debates, but you get my point here. Let's become not combative but engaged. Let's "contend for the faith" as so many in history have effectively done.

Progressives reinterpret the text with hot-button moral issues like homosexuality and abortion, but this is also true with cardinal doctrines such as the virgin birth and the bodily resurrection of Jesus. As Childers says, the only sacred cow is that there are no sacred cows. You might hear progressives say things like:

- "The resurrection of Jesus doesn't have to be factual to be true."
- "The church's position on sexuality is culture-bound, but the trajectory of Scripture teaches us to accept all sexual expressions."
- "Hell is the life we live here as inauthentic persons."

Inaccurate reinterpretations of essential Christian doctrines rob these core truths of their power and open the way for people to live however they please. The belief among progressives is that by making Christianity appear to be relevant to modern Westerners, it will flourish. Of course, the opposite is always true. Making the Christian faith look like the world only teaches people that they don't need Christianity at all. As a rather infamous politician once quipped, "Make a bargain with the devil, and you'll always be the junior partner."

4. Historic terms are inaccurately redefined

One underhanded sign that your church, school, or faith is becoming progressive is when people ostensibly affirm Christian doctrine but perform linguistic gymnastics to make doctrines mean something different than what they have historically meant.

Childers recalls asking her pastor if he believed that the Bible is divinely inspired. He answered with a confident "Yes, of course!" Later, she says, she realized that he meant something very different by the term "inspired" than what historic Christianity had meant. Sometime later, he clarified that by inspiration, he only meant that Scripture has the same kind of connection to God as do other Christian books, songs, and sermons. For this leader, inspiration meant something like "spiritually elevating." Historically, though, "inspiration" has meant that Scripture contains the very words of God—and as Paul says, "is breathed out by God" and "profitable for teaching, for reproof, for correction, and for training in righteousness" (2 Tim. 3:16-17). Paul doesn't mean that Scripture is to be corrected by God-breathed progressives; he means that *we* are to be corrected by God-breathed Scripture.

Childers points out another term that has received a major redefinition in progressivism: *love*. Once progressivism has removed love from its biblical context, it becomes simply another "catch-all term for everything non-confrontative, pleasant, and affirming." Comments you might hear from a progressive include:

- "God would never punish sinners—he is love!"
- "Sure, the Bible is authoritative, but we've misunderstood it for the first two thousand years of church history."
- "It's not our job to talk to anyone about their sin; it's our job just to love them."

Childers is spot-on with her observations here. I regularly hear progressives use biblical and orthodox terms. But I see that they have subtly shifted the meaning of these terms. Love does not mean mere "inclusion," "acceptance," or "indulgence" toward sin; rather, love means caring enough for people to bring them out of the bondage of sinful behavior.

It's not just theological progressives who do this. Political progressives have frequently done the same with legal rulings, public policies, and even the U.S. Constitution—redefining terms to mean something foreign to authorial intent, and often in contradiction to the plain meaning of terms. They seem to be unaware that playing such a game *today* will result in disasters *tomorrow*.

When theological progressives subtly shift the meaning of terms, they continue to *sound* orthodox. It even lends a sense of authority to their presentations. But by shifting the meaning of terms, progressives actually undermine their own work and teach people to be dishonest with the Christian faith. If words mean whatever we want them to mean, then they don't mean anything at all. The average college professor may be able to redefine a term and hold her job, but her students will eventually see that her lessons aren't about anything other than what she wants to be true. And they will quickly move on from *her* claims of truth to whatever it is *they* want to be true. This is, of course, what professor Barrett meant when he said to me that the Christian faith is not negotiable.

5. The heart of the gospel message shifts from sin and redemption to social justice

Childers says it well: "There is no doubt that the Bible commands us to take care of the unfortunate and defend those who are oppressed. This is a very real and profoundly important part of what it means to live out our Christian faith. However, the core message of Christianity—the gospel—is that Jesus died for our sins, was buried and resurrected, and thereby reconciled us to God. *This* is the message that will *truly* bring freedom to the oppressed."

As I've already noted, progressive Christianity began as an attempt to create an ethical system designed to bring about a virtuous civic life here and now. In such a system, the gospel of atonement is unnecessary. With human nature being what it is, whatever is unnecessary for one generation becomes anathema for the next. So progressives frequently replace the gospel of Jesus' death with a social activist message that doesn't require the death of Jesus. You hear such things as:

- "All people are basically good."
- "God doesn't require the death of Jesus for our sins—it would be unjust for God to have allowed Jesus to be killed for the sins *we* committed."
- "We don't need to preach the gospel—we just need to show love by bringing justice to the oppressed and provision to the needy."

These statements are far from benign; they have the potential to corrode apostolic faith from the inside out. The shift away from the apostolic gospel is beginning to take significant ground, and it's only growing in popularity.

The Pervasiveness of Progressivism

Theological progressivism is all around us, and because many of us are busy with life, we simply don't notice when it begins to creep into our world. Some progressives prefer it that way. I have known progressives who realize they cannot keep their audience by stating clearly what they actually believe, so they use biblical language and concepts in slippery ways.

They invite people to follow them into progressivism over a long period of time. It's often gradual, slow, and accommodating. It also tastes good because it's designed to appeal to the cultural sensitivities all around us.

Like I've said before (and shared through my experiences at Vanderbilt), progressivism typically starts in Christian colleges and universities. There, professors and administrators have the difficult job of balancing orthodoxy with rigorous academic standards and the need to fit into the larger social context around them. Christian colleges have a strong need for a *civic* religion—one that still attracts Christian students but does not offend either their students' increasingly pagan worldviews or the cultural expectations of the communities in which the colleges live. Many times, such schools will still have large religion or Bible departments, host chapel services, and speak frequently about the importance of "faith." But they simply won't offend their many constituencies by insisting upon the radical claims of biblical Christianity or by actually speaking of "Christ" rather than of mere "faith."

And so many Christian colleges and universities dilute biblical Christianity to stay alive and relevant. Recently one of the students of my church enrolled in a Christian university to begin preparations for his future career. Up to this point, much of his life had been happily faithful to the apostolic faith, yet it became threatened when his first Bible class assigned textbooks. He brought them home, and when his mother looked at the books, she became concerned and asked me for my opinion on them. The books were warmly titled *Reading the Bible Again for the First Time* (Marcus Borg) and *What is the Bible?* (Rob Bell). Though they had good-sounding titles, both books actually seek to undermine a plain reading of Scripture and replace it with a progressive vision of faith. Her question to me was this: "Do you think that either the students or their parents realize what these books are saying?" I sadly answered no.

But progressivism is not just in our schools. Many former evangelical leaders are drifting into theological progressivism too; the pressure is simply enormous. As Americans are continually bombarded with messages about inclusivity, diversity, and acceptance, biblical calls to holiness, God-defined exclusivity, and high morals seem severe and hateful. I find the members of my own church often wanting our leaders to soften the message, adapt to cultural norms, and open themselves to a hundred shades of gray.

North American evangelical leaders sometimes get punished for taking strong biblical stands, and we often get rewarded for ignoring them. Having been burned by conservative churches, many of our members want us to soften the faith and turn it into a feel-good, be-nice message.

And so we heap upon ourselves, as the apostle Paul says, teachers who scratch our itching ears (2 Tim. 4:3). We ask for teachers and authors who will tell us what we want to hear, but what we seem to neglect in this pursuit are the effects that compromise exerts upon us and our children. Compromise with the world does not make us better Christians; it makes us non-Christians. And the lives of our pagan children are the living proof of such.

Thankfully, there are still millions of Americans who want and uphold the real thing. There are numerous church leaders, college professors, and ordinary Christians who know that God's Word brings blessings which nothing else can provide. They want to follow the Jesus who is, not the Jesus decadent America wants. Some are even returning from the journey of progressivism to the power, beauty, and truthfulness of the real thing. We can make a difference if we seek to renew a biblical faith.

University professor Mary Poplin serves as an example of such a person.

An Unlikely Convert

"If you are real, please come and get me, please come and get me," said Mary Poplin.

She was an unlikely convert. A well-respected, tenured professor in an elite university, Mary Poplin had grown up in a left-leaning church. But all that remained from her early church faith were strong desires for social reform, spiritual experimentation, and personal fulfillment. So by the time she was middle-aged, Poplin was following the well-worn path of progressivism. She experimented with Buddhism and Zen meditation, developed radical feminist and Marxist convictions, and joined various causes of social justice. Along with many of her colleagues, she advocated for free love, post-modernism, secularism, and revolution. She also explored the darker side of some forms of progressivism—the abuses of alcohol, sex, and drugs—as well as the occult. She went through two divorces and aborted the lives of several of her babies.

Poplin had absorbed progressivism's anti-authoritarian calls for self-fulfillment and inclusiveness, and smugly considered herself smarter, more open-minded, and more enlightened than her conservative counterparts. "In actuality," she later confessed, "I was foolish, closed-minded, confused, depressed, anxious, arrogant, and filled with darkness."[27]

Three things conspired to change her life. First, she developed a friendship with a biblical graduate student. He was different than Christians she'd encountered before. Even when sitting in her radical leftist classes, he conducted himself with Christian conviction and love, and every project she shared with him seemed wildly successful. He never tired of asking her two important questions: "When you need spiritual help, will you call me?" and "Do you believe in evil?" Both questions haunted her, but they eventually led her to biblical Christianity.

Second, Poplin had a dream in which she and all of humanity stood in line to meet Jesus at the day of judgment. As her turn came, Jesus looked deep into her eyes. She explains what happened next: "I suddenly have an awareness of every cell in my body and that every cell in my body is filled with filth. I can no longer look at him, and I fall at his feet and begin to weep." But rather than condemning her, in the dream Jesus reached out and took her by the shoulders in love. She felt a peace she had never felt before. Poplin awoke crying and called a friend to share what she had just experienced.

Third, Poplin spent several months working with Mother Teresa in Calcutta. Like her progressive friends, Poplin had already considered herself "spiritual," by which she meant "a good person." Regardless of how much her personal life was a mess, she had supported liberal social causes and received the congratulations of her colleagues for it. But like other progressives, she had an aversion to the authority of Scripture, of the church, and of religion. Watching Mother Teresa work under those authorities changed her heart. One day, she heard the missionary say that the work in Calcutta is not social work. Rather, the nun explained, it is religious work for God. Poplin's eyes were opened.

God pursued Mary Poplin and brought her to authentic Christianity—the kind where Jesus is not a mere social worker but is Lord and

Savior; where the Bible is not a pick-and-choose collection of metaphors but the breathing Word of God; where holiness is not another form of enslavement but a beautiful lifestyle; and where the church is no longer the problem but a community of people working toward the solution.

She began reading the Bible, praying, and attending church services. At one service, the pastor invited anyone who was willing to believe in Jesus to take communion with the congregation. "When the pastor said this, I was strongly drawn to receive communion but being at the back of the church, we had to wait for our chance to go forward," Poplin remembers. "I thought to myself that even if a tornado rips through this building, I am going to get that communion. I went forward and knelt at the rail, took the bread and grape juice, bowed my head and said, 'If you are real, please come and get me, please come and get me.'"

Mary Poplin became a biblical disciple in 1993. She remained a professor at Claremont Graduate University in California, where she was director of the Teacher Education Program and Dean of the School of Educational Studies. She has made important contributions to the subject of integrating faith and academics, understanding the failures of secularism, and reducing the achievement gaps between students of different races. Plus, she lives in the beauty, power, and truth of biblical Christianity.

One of the most photographed buildings in the world is the Leaning Tower of Pisa. Completed in the 13th century, the marble building has nearly 300 steps to the top, is surrounded by gorgeous Corinthian columns, and plays seven bells. The façade is lovely, and the building is today a UNESCO World Heritage site. But even as it was being constructed 800 years ago, it began to tilt. Today the alignment at its top is more than twelve feet off, and the building is sinking too. Several efforts have been made to rectify the tower; some have helped, others have actually made it worse.

The problem is its foundation. The tower was built on sandy ground rather than on solid rock.

Jesus warns us about foundations. If we build on a solid foundation, our work will last. But if we build on faulty foundations, our work will collapse (Matt. 7:21-27). The only foundation for the Christian mission, as Jesus says, is the Word of God. Redefining Scripture, downplaying its harder parts, and forcing it to submit to our own cultural preferences will weaken its foundation. One day the Tower of Pisa will fall. That is, unless someone rebuilds its foundation. No one will do this because it's an artifact. The church today is on its way toward becoming an artifact too, but it's not too late. Like the Tower, progressivism—that massive enterprise of Western liberalism—is going to collapse. Only those who have built their lives on the Word of God will stand.

And so it is to the authority of the Word of God that we must now turn.

Chapter 3
Battling Over the Bible

On July 21, 1863, Robert and Caroline Thomas set sail for China from the unfortunately named town of Gravesend, England. Robert, a Welshman whose Christian heart had been set aflame for foreign missions, had a vision for reaching the Chinese for Christ. After a four-month journey, the young couple arrived in China. Things did not go well for them. Within a few months of their arrival, Caroline died while giving birth. Unsanitary conditions, disease, and opposition took their toll on Robert.

Taking up residency near Beijing, the widowed Robert heard that there were thousands of Christians, who had been persecuted for years, in the Hermit Kingdom of Korea. Determined to evangelize in Korea, Robert twice boarded ships and crossed the Yellow Sea, distributing Bibles and speaking the gospel to anyone who dared to listen. On his second voyage, the merchant ship he had boarded became embroiled in a firefight with Korean soldiers, and eventually the ship sank. Many were killed on both sides, and Robert was captured and executed. He was 27 years old at the time of his death.

Seeing this man's resolve and goodness, many Koreans became interested in Christ. In spite of government efforts to destroy the Bibles he had distributed, many hid their new Bibles and read them in secret. One who kept his Bible was a government official who tore out the pages of the Bible and used it to paper the walls of his house. Before long, people were lining up at his house to read the Scriptures. Soon, they were becoming followers of Jesus simply by reading this official's wallpaper. Churches began to be planted. A Christian ember was stoked. When news of the Great Welsh Revival came to Korea in 1905, the Christian faith exploded into flames—the great Pyongyang Revival. Thousands became followers of Jesus, and they planted hundreds of churches. Today, Korea is the most Christian nation in Asia, and Korean Christians are among the most prayerful and serious Christians on the planet.

Americans don't know the name of Robert Jermain Thomas, and even the Welsh have generally forgotten him. But ask any Korean Christian, or for that matter any Korean, who Robert Jermain Thomas is, and they can tell you. He is the man who brought us the Bible and changed our culture. The Bible, pasted to the walls of a government bureaucrat's house, helped spark a spiritual revolution in Korea. As the Bible says about itself: "… the word of God is living and active, sharper than any two-edged sword …" (Heb. 4:12). This is the power of the Bible. It has the power to change hearts, overcome addictions and enslavement, and change towns, cities, and whole nations. More than any other book, it formed Western civilization, and it undergirds all that is Christian.

Because progressivism undermines the Christian Bible, it cuts itself off from the power of God and his Word. Indeed, if Koreans had been given the theological positions of liberal progressives rather than the Bible, no revival would have broken out. Don't misunderstand: the Korean government would still have bitterly opposed the message but not because of the biblical message of salvation. Rather, they would have rejected it for its decadent North American values. They would have rejected it as too pagan rather than as too Christian. If left to progressives, there would never have been a Pyongyang Revival.

The Battle Over the Bible

One of the main differences between historic, orthodox Christianity and progressivism is the view of the Bible each holds. Historic Christianity has always looked on the apostolic treasure as the very Word of God, the foundation of our truths, and our way of life. Progressivism has a low view of Scripture, often submitting Scriptures to contemporary tastes—shown in statements like those mentioned in the previous chapter (e.g., "The Bible is a human book written by human authors").

Since our view of the Bible is fundamental to how we talk about the Christian faith, even before we discuss who Jesus is, we must address questions that revolve around this defining source of information about Jesus and the Christian faith. There's really no way to talk about Jesus without first determining the nature and authority of the Bible. This is true even though many of us have a daily supra-biblical relationship with Jesus that fills our hearts and our lives. We would have no vocabulary to describe our experience of Jesus were it not for the Bible; we wouldn't even be able to name it.

For this reason, we must start with the Bible. And everyone who is informed about the nature of progressivism knows that, ultimately, theological progressivism is a question of religious authority. Will we define the Christian faith using the Christian Bible as our source of authority—complemented by Christianity's richest teachers, the great creeds of the faith, and the witness of the worldwide church? Or will we submit the Christian faith to our own sentiments, our own flawed reason, and the passions of our ever-changing experiences? This is the critical choice. You can follow the teachings of the Bible, given by the prophets and apostles who actually lived with Jesus. Or you can follow your own sentiments, constantly being fashioned by American myths of progress and political interests. You cannot follow both.

Now, we must admit that there is a certain historical distance between ourselves and the Bible, and that there are many difficult questions about the Bible. This is true even for those of us who want to follow its teachings.

Before exploring these questions, however, we must say that many progressives do not really reject the Bible because of these questions. Rather, progressives tend to reject the Bible because they have been told that it doesn't conform to their self-authenticating sensibilities.[28] People reject the Bible because they don't want it to be true. They prefer their own interpretations of reality, and the Bible refuses to conform to these preferences. In her book on biblical inspiration, Rachel Held Evans argues that the Bible is intended to *ask* questions rather than to *answer* them. Her position is soothing to North American ears, but at the end of the day, all it really means is that *we* get to decide which parts of the Bible are true and which are not.

Richard Rohr gives us a different spin on the authority of Scripture. He suggests that we compare the Bible with people we admire, like, or those in whom we believe. If the Bible is not as good as these people, we should be suspicious of the Bible. Here's how he puts it: "If you are meditating on a Bible text, Hebrew or Christian, and if you see God operating at a lesser level than the best person you know, then that text is not authentic revelation …. It is as simple as that."[29] I appreciate that Rohr is more open about his standard than some. He clearly says it: *we* get to decide whether or not a text of Scripture is authentic, based on *our* sentiments.

If you decide that progressive sentiments are more authoritative than Scripture, it really doesn't matter afterwards what argument you use to reject Scripture. Once you've decided that you are your own god, you don't need any further reason to reject the one true God because any explanation will do.[30]

What the Bible Says About Itself

Since the Bible is the fulcrum for how we interpret the Christian faith, it's imperative that we hear what the Bible says about itself. If we reject the Bible as the inspired and perfect Word of God, let's at least know that we are denying the claims it makes about itself. Unbelievers will reject Scripture as hopelessly antiquated, full of errors, misogynistic, anti-gay, violent, and foolish. But when progressive Christians say the same things, they should know that they are undermining the very Christian faith they claim to save. And when progressives challenge the Bible as the inspired Word of God, they contradict the actual claims of the Bible. They are essentially saying that the Bible lies about its own authority.

So what does the Bible say about itself?

The answer is complex and could easily be flattened to the point of misrepresentation, but the simple truth is that the authors and compilers of Scripture thought they were writing down the very words of God. You can reject their claims, but it's foolish to accept some of their material as divine, while rejecting the material you don't like. If the authors of the Bible thought they were recording God's Word, and they were wrong, why bother accepting *anything* they say?

Take Paul as an example. It's not uncommon to hear progressives suggest that the apostle Paul was wrong on several theological points. But many of them will go on to say that Paul was at least right about grace.[31] Paul himself claims that he got his message directly from Jesus, suggests he went to heaven and heard God's revelation, clearly states that his teachings constitute the very Word of God, and condemns those who disagree with him. If Paul cannot get his theology straight on gender, sexual orientation, Israel, holiness, or other important considerations, why would we trust him on other matters such as grace? He is deceived, he is wrong, or worse, he's evil. You can take Paul or you can leave him, but you are playing a fool's game if you take some of what he says and reject the rest as deceit.

So what else does the Bible say about itself?

Old Testament Claims

Let's start with the Old Testament. It's a simple fact that various books in our Old Testament claim to possess the very words of God. More than 800 times the Old Testament uses the formulaic phrase: "The LORD says …" The phrase is a technical one; that is, it means to qualify the accompanying quotation as the exact and very words of God. Those who wrote, "Thus says the LORD" certainly thought they were giving us the very words of God. Here are a few examples:

Moses and Aaron went and said to Pharaoh, *"Thus says the LORD,* the God of Israel, 'Let my people go, that they may hold a feast to me in the wilderness'" (Exod. 5:1). The author of the Book of Exodus believed that Moses and Aaron were real flesh-and-blood people, that the Israelites really existed and were in bondage, that the ten plagues actually happened, that the Exodus was real, and that their record of events constitutes the very words of God. If you, due to your disbelief in miracles or your disdain for violence or whatever, claim these things never happened—regardless of how you rationalize your interpretation of Exodus—you should at least know that you're disregarding what the writing actually says about itself.

> Samuel said to Saul, "The LORD sent me to anoint you
> king over his people Israel; now therefore listen to the
> words of the LORD. *Thus, says the LORD of hosts,* 'I have

noted what Amalek did to Israel in opposing them on the
way when they came up out of Egypt. Now go and strike
Amalek and devote to destruction all that they have.'"
(1 Sam. 15:1-3)

Again, you may choose to deny that God actually spoke these words.
You may choose to say they are hopelessly violent and unworthy of God.
You may choose to believe they are not consistent with your experience of
or sensibilities about God. But you may *not* legitimately say that some of
Samuel's words are from God while others are not. The Bible itself simply
won't allow you to make this claim.

There are hundreds of other examples. Your science may lead you to
deny Jeremiah's claim that God says he is the creator of the universe (Jer.
44:24). Your doubts about the divinity of Christ may lead you to deny Isaiah's claim that God personally prophesies the virgin birth (Isa. 7:14 with
Matt. 1:23). Your doubts about how God acts among humans may lead
you to deny the biblical claim that God personally opens *and* shuts wombs
(Isa. 66:9), that God personally condemns the worship of any other god
(Jer. 2:22ff.), that God personally condemns sexual sin (Jer. 5:8-9), and so
on. You may deny that God says these things, but you should know that
the authors of the Bible didn't doubt that God said them. They recorded
these words under the conviction that they were recording the very words
of God.

This conviction permeates the Old Testament. The prophets of justice
(progressives tend to believe the prophets) built their prophetic texts upon
the premise that the legal and narrative portions of the Scripture preced-
ing their works are true, right, and inspired. This is why they regularly call
people *back* to the Torah, as opposed to *forward* to a different religion. You
undermine the prophets when you cut them off from the rest of the Bible
simply because you choose some of their comments about the poor but
disagree with the rest of their claims. *The very same prophets who called for
justice for the poor in the name of the Lord also called for many non-progressive
values in the name of the same Lord*—often in the very same sentences. For
example, the very same prophet who says that "to know God" is to take up
the cause of the poor also says that he will punish people for sexual sin (Jer.
22:16; see also 7:5). When you pick and choose only those sections that

agree with your most recent sensibilities, you're manipulating Scripture for your own purposes.

The Psalms elevate the Word of God and clearly state that the Old Testament writings are a sacred treasure. Psalm 19 is a good example. After joyfully declaring the revelatory power of nature in verses 1-6, the psalmist moves on to describe the perfection of the written word, with its commands, ordinances, and precepts:

> The law [Hebrew, *Torah*] of the LORD is perfect, reviving
> the soul; the testimony of the LORD is sure, making
> wise the simple; the precepts of the LORD are right,
> rejoicing the heart; the commandment of the LORD
> is pure, enlightening the eyes; the fear of the LORD is
> clean, enduring forever; the rules of the LORD are true,
> and righteous altogether. More to be desired are they than
> gold, even much fine gold; sweeter also than honey and
> drippings of the honeycomb. Moreover, by them is your
> servant warned; in keeping them there is great reward.
> (Ps. 19:7-11)

Psalm 119, the longest "chapter" in the Bible, is nothing but an acrostic hymn in praise of the written Word of God. Hear just a few of its admonitions: "Teach me, O LORD, the way of your statutes; and I will keep it to the end. Give me understanding, that I may keep your law and observe it with my whole heart. Lead me in the path of your commandments, for I delight in it" (Ps. 119:33-35).

It's worth stating again that in all these texts (and many more) the writers and compilers of the Old Testament thought they were recording and preserving the very words of God. When progressives choose parts of the Old Testament (such as the prophetic calls to justice), but reject other parts (such as warnings against sexual sin or threats of judgment), they are guilty of the worst sort of sin—elevating themselves over the Word of God.

Rather than sorting through our sentiments to assess which texts we'll accept, we are far better off embracing the attitude that God articulates in Isaiah: "This is the one to whom I will look: he who is humble and contrite in spirit and *trembles at my word*'" (Isa. 66:1-2).

New Testament Claims

The New Testament writers confirm the Old Testament's claim to be the very Word of God. Repeatedly, the New Testament refers to Old Testament texts, laws, claims, and stories as the actual Word of God. Indeed, the entire New Testament is openly built upon the Old Testament. Jesus and the original Christian movement saw themselves as the legitimate heirs of the Word of God recorded in the Hebrew Scriptures.

This explains why the New Testament authors persistently quote the Old Testament as a source of authority for their actions and their words—as many as 300 quotes and allusions to the Old Testament appear in the New Testament alone. Take the Gospel of Matthew. Chapters 1 and 2 make four references to the Old Testament as the infallible Word of God: that Jesus would be born from a virgin (1:23, referencing Isa. 7:14) in Bethlehem (2:6, referencing Mic. 5:2); that he would flee to Egypt (2:15, referencing Hos. 11:1), and that Herod would kill babies in Bethlehem (2:18, referencing Jer. 38:15). For our discussion, it doesn't really matter how Matthew interprets these Old Testament texts. What matters is that Matthew saw them as the Word of God.

The rest of the Gospels continually build upon the Old Testament as the Word of God. Jesus lives as a faithful Jew who observes the Sabbath, teaches the Old Testament in the synagogues, practices the justice taught in the Old Testament prophets, and dies according to Old Testament predictions.

From the opening chapter all the way to the last, the Book of Acts presumes the Christian faith is the rightful heir of the Old Testament (see 1:20; 28:25-28). Consider also that Luke, the author of Acts, is the same as the author of the Gospel of Luke—meaning that Luke believes the early church's practices constitute the divine example of how to live in the kingdom Jesus proclaimed.

The apostle Paul regularly argues for the validity of the Old Testament and builds his theology around it as the Word of God. In his letter to the Romans, Paul writes: "So the law is holy, and the commandment is holy and righteous and good …. For we know that the law is spiritual …" (Rom. 7:12-14). Indeed, Paul teaches us that those who put their faith in Christ actually obey the Old Testament because the entire Old Testament was written about Christ (Rom. 3:31; 8:3-4). Paul makes the point that the Old Testament was actually written for Christians because we are its heirs (1 Cor. 10:11; Rom. 15:4). The rest of the New Testament continues to build upon the conviction that the Old Testament is the Word of God—quoting it, alluding to it, and building a theology upon it.

Several New Testament texts are explicit in claiming inspiration for the Old Testament. Paul says of the Old Testament: "All Scripture is breathed out by God and profitable for teaching, for reproof, for correction, and for training in righteousness, that the man of God may be competent, equipped for every good work" (2 Tim. 3:16-17). At the beginning of his second letter, the apostle Peter reminds us: "And we have something more sure, the prophetic word, to which you will do well to pay attention as to a lamp shining in a dark place, until the day dawns and the morning star rises in your hearts, knowing this first of all, that no prophecy of Scripture comes from someone's own interpretation" (2 Pet. 1:19-20).

Jesus himself is described in the Gospels as granting authority to the Scriptures. We follow the wrong Jesus when we attempt to dissociate him from the Old Testament. After all, it was Jesus who said:

> Do not think that I have come to abolish the Law or the Prophets; I have not come to abolish them but to fulfill them. For truly, I say to you, until heaven and earth pass away, not an iota, not a dot, will pass from the Law until all is accomplished. Therefore, whoever relaxes one of the least of these commandments and teaches others to do the same will be called least in the kingdom of heaven, but whoever does them and teaches them will be called great in the kingdom of heaven. (Matt. 5:17-19)

When theological progressives belittle the Scriptures, Jesus literally says (in red letters!) that they are least in the kingdom of God.

Moreover, Jesus frequently quotes from the Old Testament, and even when he's correcting the Pharisees' misinterpretations, Jesus acknowledges its authority. Consider these examples:

- Jesus declares that Scripture cannot be broken (John 10:35).
- Jesus calls the Old Testament "the commandment of God" (Matthew 15:3).
- Jesus refers to Scripture as "the Word of God" (Mark 7:13).
- Jesus chastises the Sadducees for their partial disbelief of the Scriptures, quoting Genesis, while chiding them: "Have you not read what was said to you by God?" (Matthew 22:29-31).
- Jesus answers the temptations of Satan by quoting the Old Testament (Matthew 4:4-10).
- Jesus believes in the historicity of Adam (Matthew 19:4), Cain and Abel (Luke 11:51), Noah (Luke 17:26), Jonah (Matthew 12:40), the creation account (Mark 10:6-9), and the reality of heaven and hell (Mark 9:44-46).

Undoubtedly, Jesus was a man of the Bible. Anyone who follows Jesus will be a person of the Bible too.

To reject the authority of Scripture, whether explicitly like many progressives do, or by explaining it away like other progressives do, is to reject Jesus. If you follow Jesus, you will accept what he says about the Bible. It's really that simple.

Once we accept the authority of the Old Testament, it's not a stretch to see that the New Testament claims the same authority. Repeatedly, we read that the New Testament authors, apostles, and prophets of the early church claim they are recording the truthful words of God. This explains why the New Testament refers to its own writings as Scripture. Peter cites Paul's writings, then says of them that, "There are some things in them that are hard to understand, which the ignorant and unstable twist to their own destruction, as they do the other Scriptures" (2 Pet. 3:15-16). Peter actually calls Paul's writings "Scripture." Paul quotes from Luke 10:7 in connection with Deuteronomy 25:4, equating the authority of the two and calling both "Scripture" (1 Tim. 5:18).

This isn't surprising, since Jesus promised the apostles that they would receive the Holy Spirit, who would "guide them in all truth" by reminding them of what Jesus taught them (John 16:13). Peter not only explains that he has the Spirit but also that he is writing as an eyewitness to the truth: "For we did not follow cleverly devised myths when we made known to you the power and coming of our Lord Jesus Christ, but we were eyewitnesses of his majesty" (2 Pet. 1:16).[32]

Further, Peter reassures us that Jesus literally spoke through the apostles:

> This is now the second letter that I am writing to you,
> beloved. In both of them I am stirring up your sincere
> mind by way of reminder, that you should remember the
> predictions of the holy prophets and *the commandment of
> the Lord and Savior through your apostles*, knowing this first
> of all, that scoffers will come in the last days with scoffing,
> following their own sinful desires. (2 Pet. 3:1-3)

Luke explains that he carefully researched everything he describes in his Gospel and Acts (which together make up a quarter of the New Testament!) so that we could be certain about the Word:

> Inasmuch as many have undertaken to compile a narrative
> of the things that have been accomplished among us,
> just as those who from the beginning were eyewitnesses
> and ministers of the word have delivered them to us, it
> seemed good to me also, having followed all things closely
> for some time past, to write an orderly account for you,
> most excellent Theophilus, that you may have certainty
> concerning the things you have been taught. (Luke 1:1-4)

And Jesus clarifies the authority of the apostles when he says, "No servant is greater than his master …. If they obeyed my teaching, they will obey yours also" (John 15:20). Anyone who does not follow the apostles is not following Jesus.

So far, I've focused on the Old and New Testaments. With regard to the New Testament, most people will not contend much with some of the "red letters" of the Synoptic Gospels. But there is something about the apostle Paul and other portions of the New Testament that makes progressives recoil. Paul has become to progressives the perfect way to attack our religion. But do their arguments hold weight?

Chapter 4
The Apostle Paul and Self-Inspired Sentimentality

"To Carthage I came, burning."[33]

—T. S. Elliott

Striding like a colossus between the Roman world and the Middle Ages is the enormously influential church father Augustine.

Augustine grew up in North Africa the son of a Christian mother and a pagan father. A self-described lustful young man, Augustine tasted numerous forms of pagan delights—often encouraged by his father. By the time he was twenty-something, he already had a young son and a live-in girlfriend.

But Augustine's saintly mother, Monica, never stopped praying for him. In his early twenties, Augustine moved to Milan, where he fell under the spell of Ambrose—an eloquent preacher who challenged his congregation with calls to apostolic faithfulness.

Eventually, Augustine began to realize that God was calling him. Monica's prayers were being answered in a powerful way. Augustine's only holdback was the delight he took in sexual sin. He knew from experience what we should know today: sensual desires war against the soul (1 Pet. 2:11). "Lord," he prayed, "give me sexual self-restraint, but not yet."

Then, one day Augustine was sitting in the garden of a friend, struggling with his desire to follow Jesus but also wanting to hold on to his sinful way of life. He was in a deep state of despair. Suddenly, he heard school children next door playing a game and crying out "pick up and read, pick up and read!" Taking it as a sign from God, Augustine reached for a copy of the Christian Scripture, and the book fell open to Romans 13:14: "But put on the Lord Jesus Christ, and make no provision for the flesh, to gratify its desires."

Augustine immediately heard the voice of God in Paul's admonition. He immediately knew that his sexual sin was in the way of his relationship with God and that it was preventing him from "denying himself, taking up a cross, and following" Jesus (as Jesus had said). Reading Paul, the divine ambassador of Jesus, Augustine gave up his sinful life and became, perhaps, the greatest post-biblical teacher in Christian history. Even to this day, his works are definitive for Christian theology. Even to this day, Augustine shapes our faith.

Had Augustine not trusted the apostle Paul as a faithful ambassador for Christ, we would likely never have heard of him. In fact, had he not trusted the apostle Paul, Augustine may well have used his considerable intellectual powers to attack the Christian faith. But just as Paul faithfully followed Jesus, so Augustine faithfully followed Paul (see 1 Cor. 11:1). And the world was changed.

The Apostle Paul Among Progressives

But Paul has fallen on hard times among progressives. Even though he is Christ's divinely appointed representative, progressives simply cannot bring themselves to accept his teaching. In an interview with Oprah Winfrey, Rob Bell openly declared this. Speaking of same-sex marriage, Bell says, "[T]he church will continue to be even more irrelevant when it quotes letters from 2,000 years ago as their best defense, when you have in front of you flesh-and-blood people who are your brothers and sisters, and aunts and uncles, and co-workers and neighbors ...."[34] Bell's wife, Kristen, added that churches that don't reject Paul's teaching on sexuality are guilty of regression.

Given progressivism's modulation or even rejection of the letters of Paul, we must take some time to address Paul's authority so we can reclaim this rabbi, missionary, church planter, and inspired ambassador of Christ for the 21st century. I will reference Paul's own statements, but for a more general defense of Paul, see the excellent article by Scott McKnight, "Jesus vs. Paul."[35]

Let's start with Paul's apostolicity. Again and again, the apostle Paul claims that his teaching possesses final authority as the Word of God. A few examples:

- "And we also thank God constantly for this, that when you received the word of God, which you heard from us, you accepted it not as the word of men but as what it really is, the word of God, which is at work in you believers" (1 Thessalonians 2:13).
- "But even if we or an angel from heaven should preach to you a gospel contrary to the one we preached to you, let him be accursed. As we have said before, so now I say again: If anyone is preaching to you a gospel contrary to the one you received, let him be accursed" (Galatians 1:8–9).
- Speaking of gender roles and other matters of the gathering, Paul warns: "If anyone thinks that he is a prophet, or spiritual, he should acknowledge that the things I am writing to you are a command of the Lord. If anyone does not recognize this, he is not recognized" (1 Corinthians 14:37-38).

Paul can make these claims, which he does many more times, because the Christian church is built upon the foundation of the prophets and the apostles. Look at what he says in Ephesians and what John says about apostles in Revelation:

- "When you read this, you can perceive my insight into the mystery of Christ, which was not made known to the sons of men in other generations as it has now been revealed to his holy apostles and prophets by the Spirit" (Ephesians 3:4-5).
- "[B]ut you are ... built on the foundation of the apostles and prophets, Christ Jesus himself being the cornerstone, in whom the

whole structure, being joined together, grows into a holy temple in the Lord" (Ephesians 2:19-21).
- "The wall of the city had twelve foundations, and on them were the names of the twelve apostles of the Lamb" (Revelation 21:14).

The apostles and prophets are ambassadors of Christ, meaning that they are his ordained representatives on earth. So if we want to follow Jesus, we will submit to the teachings of his holy prophets and apostles. Those unwilling to submit to Paul's teachings (remember he's an apostle of Christ) are actually rebelling against Jesus.

Again, I am dwelling on this point because progressivism typically has a low view of the holy apostle Paul. This devaluing of Paul and his teaching isn't new. Often in his own lifetime, Paul had to defend his apostleship against those who considered themselves more spiritual, smarter, and more knowledgeable about Jesus than he. The entire last four chapters of 2 Corinthians as well as most of the book of Galatians consist of Paul's defense of himself, offered because many sought to undermine him in the 1st century.

In the 21st century, progressives tend to not like Paul's teaching for several reasons:

- Because Paul affirms complementarian gender roles in marriage and in the church.
- Because Paul affirms what the entire Bible teaches about sexual purity—anything other than one man in a married relationship with one woman is either sinful, disordered, or both.
- Because progressives don't like Paul's teaching about sin and atonement, God's justice, or the exclusivity of Christ.

There are other things that progressives dislike about Paul, so at the end of the day, for progressives, Paul has to be discredited. Note that progressives don't dismiss Paul because he is unclear or incoherent; they dismiss him because they don't *feel* like he is right. They really don't need an argument. Remember what we talked about earlier: once you decide your feelings are more authoritative than God's Word, any argument will do.

So we often hear challenges from the left about Jesus versus Paul. When everyday liberals pit Paul against Jesus, we might conclude that they're simply naïve. But when pastors, authors, bloggers, and theologians pit Jesus against Paul, it's difficult not to believe that they are deliberately deceiving people. Why? Because we don't have any writings from Jesus at all! There is no book written by Jesus to pit against the works of Paul.[36]

Educated progressives know that Jesus did not physically write a single line of Scripture, including the red-letter sections. They know that when we read Luke, we're not reading Jesus—instead, we're reading Luke's *interpretation* of Jesus, which is not the same as the interpretations of Jesus by Mark, Matthew, John, Peter, or Paul. Each book of the New Testament, including the Gospels, gives us an *interpretation* of Jesus. Educated progressives know this. So when they pit Jesus against Paul, it's difficult not to conclude that they are deliberately deceiving people to establish a different gospel.

And there's more; we must consider Paul's place in the Scriptures chronologically: Paul is *our earliest witness* to Jesus. The very first Christian writings in all of history are Paul's letters about Jesus. Best we can tell, almost all of Paul's letters were written before a single Gospel was composed. Before there were any "red letters," there was the near-complete body of Paul's works. This apostle with the radical conversion is chronologically closer to Jesus than any Gospel writer, and Paul's experience of Jesus begins within months of the resurrection.

But there's more, for it was Paul who actually trained Luke. Any "red letter" Luke recorded was, at least in part, taught to Luke by Paul. So if one quotes Luke's red letters against Paul, one is ignorantly subordinating the teacher to the student: Paul was the teacher, Luke was the student. There is no Jesus versus Paul—the Jesus of Luke was, at least in part, a product of the apostle Paul. And as Jesus says, the servant is not greater than the master. Similarly, the early church argued that the Gospel of Mark was actually compiled from the teachings of Peter.[37] So to pit the red letters of Mark against the letters of Peter is also to subordinate, again in ignorant fashion, the teacher to the student.[38] To pit either Peter or Paul (as represented in their letters) against the Gospel stories of Jesus is to violate the spirit of both.

This is an important point for many reasons, and it serves to remind us that a major strategy of progressives—the strategy of undermining the New Testament epistles by subordinating them to sections of the Synoptic

Gospels—is fallacious. Progressives often seek to drive a wedge between preferred sections of the Synoptic Gospels and the rest of the New Testament. Indeed, many tend to believe that the non-preferred writers of the New Testament actually *corrupted* the message of the Gospels. But the truth is that the Gospel writers are chronologically the *furthest* from Jesus among most of the New Testament writings, and often the Gospel writers actually received their material directly from the other New Testament authors. The apostles Paul and Peter are prior to the Gospels, as is James, the brother of Jesus. And the apostle John is at least a partial contemporary with the Synoptic authors.

Back to Paul. The apostle Paul went to heaven and received his revelation directly from God (2 Cor. 12:1-4), and God gave him the ability to perform signs, wonders, and powers of the Holy Spirit to confirm it (Rom. 15:18-19). To progressives who routinely dismiss Paul in favor of a narrow reading of Luke's or Matthew's teachings about Jesus, I ask: Don't you think that God might have mentioned something to Paul about all the errors you've discovered in Paul's writings when Paul was in God's throne room? When Paul says that he did not make up his teaching but received it directly from Jesus as a divine revelation (Gal. 1:11-12), do you think he is lying? And if he is lying, why would you follow anything a liar says?

Paul admonishes us to follow his example and even teaches us to pay attention only to those who follow the pattern he gave us (Phil. 3:17-19). He contrasts those who follow his teachings with people he calls the enemies of the cross: "Their end is destruction, their god is their belly, and they glory in their shame, with minds set on earthly things. But our citizenship is in heaven, and from it we await a Savior, the Lord Jesus Christ...." And he condemns anyone who preaches any gospel other than the one he preached (Gal. 1:6-9). When progressives tell us that Paul's theology of sin and the cross is wrong, they should at least know whom they're up against.

One more thing about Paul. This apostle has taken it on the chin by any number of doubters in history. But apart from Jesus himself, nobody is more responsible for creating a worldwide movement of the kingdom of God than Paul. He traveled hundreds of miles, established numerous churches, taught thousands of disciples, and carried burdens beyond measure. Defending himself against *1st-century* scoffers, Paul explains:

I am talking like a madman—with far greater labors, far more imprisonments, with countless beatings, and often near death. Five times I received at the hands of the Jews the forty lashes less one. Three times I was beaten with rods. Once I was stoned. Three times I was shipwrecked; a night and a day I was adrift at sea; on frequent journeys, in danger from rivers, danger from robbers, danger from my own people, danger from Gentiles, danger in the city, danger in the wilderness, danger at sea, danger from false brothers; in toil and hardship, through many a sleepless night, in hunger and thirst, often without food, in cold and exposure. And, apart from other things, there is the daily pressure on me of my anxiety for all the churches. Who is weak, and I am not weak? Who is made to fall, and I am not indignant? (2 Cor. 11:23-29)

The holy apostle Paul received his teaching directly from Jesus, suffered greatly for it, and then was martyred because of it. Those who belittle him should compare the sacrifices *they've* made for the kingdom to those made by the apostle Paul—our brother, our teacher, and a foundation stone in our movement.

The sad reality is that many have simply decided that their sentiments and feelings are more important than the God-given authority of his holy apostles. Paul knew a thousand times more about Jesus than you know. He knew a thousand times more about Jesus than your pastor, your professor, and all the authors and bloggers today know—*combined*. Maybe we should allow God's holy apostle to teach us what Christ sent him to teach. Maybe we should try the real thing.

The Bible claims to be the Word of God. It is fitting, therefore, that Scripture closes with a warning in the book of Revelation: "I warn everyone who hears the words of the prophecy of this book: if anyone adds to them, God will add to him the plagues described in this book, and if anyone takes away from the words of the book of this prophecy, God will take away his share in the tree of life and in the holy city, which are described in this book" (Rev. 22:18-19).

Sentimental, Self-Inspired Theology

Those who reject the authority of the works of Paul and the rest of Scripture, regardless of how they get there, undermine their own faith. Many paths meander through progressivism and ultimately out the door of Christianity. But the most common, as we have suggested, is a dependence upon feelings and sentiments rather than upon the facts of the apostolic witness. As I mentioned earlier, you can hear feelings subtly being elevated over facts in the comments that progressives make:

- "That verse of Scripture just doesn't resonate with me."
- "I thought homosexuality was a sin until I met and befriended some gay people."
- "Jesus just wouldn't send people to hell."

There are other ways, and we must at least be aware of them. Some argue that the Scriptures are mere human products. While it's true that holy men people actually wrote down Scriptures, Peter assures us that they wrote while being "carried along by the Holy Spirit" (2 Pet. 1:20-21). And Paul explains that the inspiration process resulted in inspired books. This makes both the process of biblical composition and the biblical compositions themselves the very Word of God. We shouldn't ignore the human dimension of Scripture; after all, God uses humans to accomplish his will all the time. But we also must not ignore the divine quality of Scripture—the authors wrote what the Spirit inspired them to write.

In the last fifteen years or so, a common method for negotiating uncomfortable biblical texts is to propose a so-called "trajectory of Scripture," sometimes called a "redemptive hermeneutic," a view made popular by William Webb.[39] The argument goes something like this: The authors of Scripture recorded truth insofar as they were able to grasp it in their limited social contexts. But they planted seeds that will lead to new understandings and truths—seeds that we should cultivate and nourish into full growth. For example, the argument goes, given the social world of Paul, it was inconceivable to him that women should have the same roles as men in church, so the apostle proscribed certain duties for women. But the same apostle planted the seeds of full gender equality in such texts as Galatians 3:28 ("neither male nor female"). As smart moderns, we will dismiss Paul's proscriptions against women as culture-bound, and fully implement the freedom implied in his egalitarian-sounding statement.

There are more conservative versions of trajectory hermeneutics, but it's suspicious that most practitioners of "trajectory hermeneutics" consistently end up affirming North American, 21st-century progressive perspectives. For this reason, "trajectory hermeneutics" often turns out to be little more than another way of decoupling ourselves from the Scriptures as the Word of God.

It's true that there is a progression of revelation in the Bible from Genesis to Christ. But the New Testament teaches that this progression is finalized in Christ himself. In other words, with the work of the inspired apostles, the New Testament actually constitutes the final redemptive interpretation of revelation.[40] Any "trajectory" that conflicts with clear statements of the Bible must be rejected because no matter how elegantly they are stated, such trajectories are really nothing other than an attempt to replace biblical teaching with contemporary sensibilities. The authors of Scripture actually did understand what they were saying and they understood the implications of their words.

This leads us to the question of infallibility. Most progressives deny the infallibility of Scripture, that is, the doctrine that the Scriptures are without error—either subtly or often explicitly. Again, for the average progressive, the argument is not really based on a close reading of Scripture. Rather, it's based on the need to justify progressive disagreements with Scripture. Well-educated progressives can point to tensions, historical implausibilities, strange claims, and pre-modern assumptions in the Bible. They typically cite these issues as reasons to ignore or reimagine sections of Scripture. But it's odd that progressives only dismiss the sections of Scripture that disagree with their largely white, elite views. If so much of the Scripture is wrong, why stop with the texts that disagree with the most recent values of North American elites? Why not keep the texts that agree with people from Asia, Africa, or Latin America and dismiss the texts that agree with North American elites?

One short example. Several years back I was talking about the book of Jonah with a brother in East Africa. Among North American elites, Jonah's message of God's mercy to strangers is accepted as gospel truth, but his story of the big fish is laughed out of town; the opposite was true in East

Africa. The brother in my conversation lived in nature, fished for a living, and had experienced all kinds of outdoor things that defy explanation. He believed that Jonah was swallowed by a whale. What he couldn't accept was Jonah's call for accepting the stranger. Many of his tribe had, after all, been tormented by strangers from other tribes. So in North American coffee shops and lecture halls, where most have never actually seen a big fish, the whale part of Jonah is dismissed, but the part about including strangers—which feels so good to Western elites—is embraced with applause. The cultural imperialism here is actually astonishing. Only the parts of Jonah's story that meet the approval of Westerners should be accepted, while the experience of Africans are laughed out of the room.

Reformed pastor and author Tim Keller points out the assumptions of cultural (and I would add racial) superiority implicit in this approach to Scripture—every single solution to apparent problems in Scripture suspiciously confirms the values of white North Americans.[41] To expand upon Keller's argument, take the example of hell and the justice of God. North American white middle and upper-middle class people have always been on the winning side of justice, so the concept of a God who punishes humans for real evil is largely inconceivable to most progressives. But many people in the world (including lower class Americans) have often lived lives among great injustices. To these people, bereft of true justice and subject to daily mistreatment, hell makes perfect sense. Indeed, for much of the world, the idea of a just God is good news—and so is the belief in a new creation that does not include their tormenters. For Christians who live under Muslim dhimmitude in Pakistan, for women in Saudi Arabia, for Jewish survivors of the Holocaust, for children living in America's inner cities—for all of these and many more people, justice makes perfect sense. The biblical doctrine of the justice of God is generally incomprehensible only to those who have lived privileged lives.

When progressives evaluate Scripture based on their own values, they are actually practicing just one more form of cultural imperialism. As Keller asks regarding biblical Christianity in general, "Why should western cultural sensibilities be the final court in which to judge whether Christianity is valid?"[42]

If the Scriptures are the very Word of God, they are perfect. This is what the term infallibility typically means. Even though the Scriptures were written by human hands, they claim to be the Word of God, inspired by the Spirit of God. This means that they cannot be wrong, for God himself is never wrong. Marcus Borg argues that the doctrine of infallibility has only been around for the last half-millennium.[43] But this claim is misleading. The *term* "infallible" may be recent, but that's because it has only recently been an issue. The early church fathers, Orthodox churches, and the worldwide church have always believed that the Scriptures are the perfect Word of God.[44] The only reason debates about infallibility are relatively new is because it was only recently that Christians began to deny infallibility. Progressives have built elaborate systems to undermine the age-old Christian view of the infallibility of Scripture. Then, when orthodox Christians have sought to defend infallibility, progressives accuse them of inventing the doctrine. It's like the man who picked a fight with his wife, then divorced her for arguing.

The Bible does indeed have tensions, historical implausibilities, and theological and cultural difficulties. I'm inclined to think that those who deny this probably haven't actually read the Bible. But the solution to such problems—for those who have chosen to follow the Jesus who accepted the Bible—is to commit prayerfully to listening, submitting, and obeying the Bible, even when it doesn't fully make sense to us.[45] Our minds are broken, and our wills tend toward the self-serving. The Bible is not going to make full sense to broken humans. Indeed, if sensibility were the measurement of the truth claims of Jesus and the apostles, we wouldn't need *any* Scripture. And if we have learned anything about progressivism, it's that the movement is ever-changing and often contradicting itself.[46] It has had successes, but it has also had some disastrous failures.

Psychologist Robert Cialdini studied how persuasion and influence work in a variety of areas of life. His work helps us understand how progressivism has coupled itself to the changing social norms of North Americans. Unsure of the biblical claims, progressives look around themselves to see what others believe. When they do this, they redefine their beliefs in order to match the biblical ignorance of unbelievers in what Cialdini calls "pluralistic ignorance." I'll let him explain:

> In general, when we are unsure of ourselves, when the situation is unclear or ambiguous, when uncertainty

> reigns, we are most likely to look to and accept the
> actions of others as correct. Especially in an ambiguous
> situation, the tendency for everyone to be looking to
> see what everyone else is doing can lead to a fascinating
> phenomenon called "pluralistic ignorance."[47]

Progressives find much of the Scriptures to be out of step with what they think must be true. In their uncertainty, they look to secular thought-shapers and seek to adopt their viewpoints. They play into "pluralistic ignorance." But what they don't realize is that secular thought-shapers are also merely looking to others to see what *they* think too. Of course, as Christians, our task is not to look to secular thinkers to determine what the Christian faith is. Rather, we should treat Scripture as a compass for following Jesus, even when our instincts are telling us to go another way. Obedience is the best hermeneutic when it comes to the Bible.[48]

And so we must say this clearly. Even with its difficulties, when one chooses to follow Jesus, one chooses to accept the Bible—the Torah, the writings, the prophets, and the apostolic witnesses. Jesus was a man of the Bible. To follow Jesus, we must accept the Bible too. The Christian religion is not plastic. It is not moldable to any value system that comes along. It actually stands for something, and we should expect that various cultures are going to disagree with it. Better to be a pagan who rejects the Christian faith than a Christian who changes it to fit their self-directed sentimentalities.

Mahatma Gandhi is reported to have once remarked, "You Christians look after a document containing enough dynamite to blow all civilization to pieces, turn the world upside down, and bring peace to a battle-torn planet, but you treat it as though it is nothing more than a piece of good literature." I've seen the power of the Bible to save marriages, end addictions, rescue children, overthrow unjust structures, and restore health and well-being. But if you want that kind of biblical power, you must first believe the Bible.

And when we accept the authority of the Christian Scriptures, we see a Jesus who is powerful, beautiful, and divine. We meet the King of kings and the Lord of lords. To this subject we turn in the next chapter.

Chapter 5
The Challenge of Jesus

"I would catch a glimpse of the cross ... and suddenly my heart would stand still and in an instinctive, intuitive way, I understood that something more important, more tumultuous, more passionate, was at issue than our good causes, however noble they may be. I should have worn it. It should have been my uniform, my language, my life. I shall have no excuse, I can't say I didn't know. I knew from the beginning and turned away."[49]

Thus wrote Malcolm Muggeridge—former atheist, smoker, womanizer, groper, cynic, Marxist, and liberal—but now changed by the Lordship of Jesus.

Muggeridge was born in 1903 to a middle-class family in England. They went to a congregational church, but socialism was their real religion. So after graduating from Cambridge University, Muggeridge became a liberal journalist who worked tirelessly for left-leaning causes in every venue of life. Staunchly anti-capitalist, Muggeridge even went to the Soviet Union, which he considered the only real alternative to capitalist economics. What he saw there totally disillusioned him and planted seeds that would later change his whole life. Soviet socialism was brutal, vengeful, and murderous. Millions were killed for the sake of its socialist utopia. Muggeridge tried to communicate this to the West, but most liberals ignored him—socialism's evils simply didn't fit the narrative the left wanted to be true.

After only a few months, Muggeridge slipped out of the U.S.S.R. He served in the British military during the second war, and afterwards began a successful career as a magazine editor and TV personality. He interviewed everybody from Billy Graham to Winston Churchill.

By the late 1960s, Muggeridge was beginning to see the havoc that the left's sexual revolution was wreaking on people's lives—broken homes, abandoned children, mental illness, civil instability, and the like. Along with the rise of illegal drug use, also made popular by progressives, he began to speak and write like a Christian, turning the left even more staunchly against him. Muggeridge was beginning to see the gullibility of his youth, the misguidedness of his ideals, and the emptiness of his atheism. By 1971, he'd had enough of his pagan past and declared himself a practicing orthodox Christian. A visit to Mother Teresa convinced him that what his heart had been longing for could not be satisfied with hedonism, self-discovery, mere social justice, or anything like it. Rather, Muggeridge discovered, he needed a Savior. He needed a Lord. He needed the cross.

Muggeridge renounced his past and took up a life of service to Christ. He authored books on Jesus as Lord, argued for a biblical form of Christianity, and sought to influence the destiny of declining churches. Muggeridge largely blamed the decline of the West on the collapse of orthodox Christianity and the rise of liberalism: "Previous civilizations have been overthrown from without by the incursion of barbarian hordes. Christendom has dreamed up its own dissolution in the minds of its own intellectual elite. Our barbarians are home produced, indoctrinated at public expense, urged on by the media, dismantling Christendom."

Before he died, Muggeridge was accepted into the Roman Catholic Church, which he found most closely mirrored his convictions regarding orthodoxy. He grew increasingly pessimistic about the West, but he saw its decline as a strategy that Christ could and would use to call people to his Lordship. One of his last essays explains:

> Let us then as Christians rejoice that we see around us on
> every hand the decay of the institutions and instruments
> of power, see intimations of empires falling to pieces,
> money in total disarray, dictators and parliamentarians
> alike nonplussed by the confusion and conflicts which

encompass them. For it is precisely when every earthly hope has been explored and found wanting, when every possibility of help from earthly sources has been sought and is not forthcoming, when every recourse this world offers, moral as well as material, has been explored to no effect, when in the shivering cold the last twig has been thrown onto the fire and in the gathering darkness every glimmer of light has finally flickered out; it is then that Christ's hand reaches out sure and firm.[50]

Some of Muggeridge's estimations about the future of the West have turned out to be near-prophetic. But it's his solution to our problems that interests me. Muggeridge understood that if Jesus was a mere social activist, such as Mahatma Gandhi (whom Muggeridge personally knew), the Christian faith is worthless. The only Jesus worth knowing is the Son of God who lived a perfect life, died an atoning death, was raised as Lord over creation, offers to save those who trust him, and will return with a new creation in final judgment.

This is the Jesus of orthodox, biblical, and historic Christianity.

Jesus, Yes, But Not the Son of God

For progressive Christians, essential Christian doctrines are always open for reinterpretation. This is because progressives see themselves as, well, the bearers of progress. And so the orientation of progressivism is toward people's contemporary desires, self-affirmations, and utopic ambitions, rather than toward the apostolic treasure given to us in Scripture and historic Christianity. There are no sacred cows in progressivism. So even the person of Jesus remains negotiable for progressives, who are willing to redefine Jesus in order to make him in their own image. This is why the Jesus of progressivism is much more like an angry social policy advocate than the actual Son of God. Progressive John Pavlovitz says it succinctly: "It is not a betrayal of Jesus to live as an activist. It is in fact an embracing of his very heart. There is much to be outraged about in these days, so let yourself be outraged …. In the name of Jesus, go forth and p*ss off the wolves wherever they show up …."[51]

Progressivism has always been unnerved by the idea that Jesus is God incarnate, that he died on the cross to atone us of our sins, that he was literally raised from the dead as King of kings, and that he is going to return to judge humanity and establish a new creation. And so liberal progressives have consistently deemphasized or dismissed these non-negotiable Christian truths.

As early as the 19th century, New England liberals were rebelling against their Calvinist ancestors, who embraced a view of human nature with original sin and therefore emphasized the necessity of the atoning work of Jesus. Early precursors of progressivism such as Thomas Priestly, William Ellery Channing, and Ralph Waldo Emerson had come to believe in the basic goodness of humans. They pushed back against what they considered to be the horrors of Calvinism. Their experience among the upper-class elites and university lights of the Northeast simply would not align with the dark views of human nature held by Boston's Puritan ancestors.

Rather, preferring imagination, sentiment, and intuition over revelation and church dogma, liberals immediately began dismissing the church's doctrine of the Trinity, the divinity of Jesus, and the need for atonement. These Christian orthodoxies were not necessary, they argued; they were not intrinsic to the Christian faith, and they did not support the emerging liberal view of Jesus as a social reformer and teacher of civic ethics. The claim that Jesus is divine eventually undermines the universalism desired by progressives—if Jesus is divine, then his religion is the only right religion—a belief that theological liberals find offensive. And if Jesus' death atones for our sin, then humans are not basically good. Established Christian truths such as the Trinity, the divinity of Christ, and the atoning work of the cross all had to be denied for progressivism to flourish.

Thus, theological liberalism became Unitarian from its earliest days. According to liberals, Jesus is not divine. His death does not atone. He is not returning to judge. Rather, according to liberals, Jesus is a great teacher of virtue, justice, self-fulfillment, and ethics. He is a social reformer who models inclusiveness, kindness, tolerance, and justice. And his religion is one of ethics, not of doctrine, belief, or institutions. So the death of Jesus is not a matter of atonement. Rather, liberals argue, it's more like a martyrdom—or a mistake, or a tragedy.[52]

Even Catholic progressives, such as Richard Rohr, want to downplay Jesus' divinity. In an interview in 2011, Rohr argued that Jesus is a created being who is only 2,000 years old. Further, he argues, Jesus is not the same as Christ. But even Christ, Rohr argues, is only as old as the universe: "The Big Bang is the birth of the Christ," he says. Rohr claims that only some, including he and the mystics, have understood this—it has been forgotten by almost all Christians throughout history. Rohr's interest in advancing this claim becomes clear shortly into his interview, when he explains that it opens the door for interfaith dialogue. Though he doesn't explicitly say it, Rohr appears to mean exactly what other Universalists mean: because Jesus is only a created being, he is not the only way. All religions offer us a path to God.[53]

Robin Meyers, an American pastor and prolific proponent of progressive Christianity, more explicitly summarizes the liberal view of Jesus for 21st-century readers:

> Jesus did not come to die, rendering his life and teaching secondary. He died because of his life and teachings. He was killed for the things that he said and did. Then the claim of his first followers and his first community is that God raised him from the dead to undo the injustice done to him and to place a divine stamp of approval on his words and deeds .... Placing all the emphasis on the saving effect of the death of Christ as a cosmic bargain negates the life of Jesus.[54]

Meyers is emphatic that preaching the apostolic message of the deity of Christ and his atoning death will actually *kill* the church—in spite of the fact the Meyer's own denomination is now headed for life-support while biblical Christianity is exploding by hundreds of millions across the globe. Even the resurrection, Meyers claims, should not be taken literally. The body of Jesus, he suggests, could well have been eaten by dogs and birds. Meyers can say all this because he is also adamant that the parts of Scripture that disagree with him are flatly wrong. A few of the chapter titles of Meyers's book *Saving Jesus From the Church* state the current liberal position succinctly: "Jesus the Teacher, Not the Savior," "Faith as Being,

Not Belief," "The Cross as Futility, Not Forgiveness," and "Religion as Relationship, Not Righteousness." One can only wonder why anyone would bother to follow a Jesus whose biographies are unreliable, whose appointed ambassadors were deceived, whose death has no meaning, and whose body was eaten by dogs—but Meyers is excited to preach such a progressive Jesus to a denomination that has lost half of its members in the last few decades under such preaching.

The Gospel of Atonement

It's important here to see what's going on in theological progressivism. In the last hundred years or so, discussions about the Trinity, the nature of Christ, and substitutionary atonement are often not really about these doctrines at all. They are rather questions about the essential character of the Christian religion.

Orthodox biblical Christianity unambiguously states that humans are fallen in sin and incapable of saving themselves. Because of our sin, each of us is separated from God and deserves to be punished. But in his great mercy, God became human in the person of Jesus, took our sins upon himself, and bore our punishment on the cross. Rising from the dead, Jesus is now the King of kings, and he calls people everywhere to repent of their personal sin, take up their cross, and follow him. And he is going to return, raise the dead, judge humanity, banish the unrepentant, and establish a new creation.

Theological liberals proclaim a different religion. In their vision, humans are inherently *good*, not sinful. Jesus is *not* God in the flesh. Rather, he is merely a man anointed by God to show us a better way to live. Since we humans are not inherently sinful, they argue, Jesus doesn't atone for our sins. And his ministry is not concerned with personal repentance, forgiveness of sins, and holy living. Richard Rohr, in the article referenced above, goes to great length to deny the atoning nature of Jesus' death.[55] His argument is not based on Scripture. Rather, it is based on his sheltered belief that humans are too good to need atoning—a view very much at home in North American elite circles but hardly in line with the experiences of vast numbers of oppressed humans around the world.

So for progressives, Jesus is an activist in the image of modern Western progressivism who brings about social reform characterized by tolerance, acceptance, and the affirmations of others. Jesus did not die for our sins; instead, he died because the Roman and Jewish authorities could not tolerate his message of social justice. Jesus was not literally raised from the dead. Rather, the resurrection is metaphorical; it is a witness to the slow and unrelenting victory of progressive values. And Jesus is not coming again to judge humanity; nobody will go to hell. Rather, we will build our own heavenly utopia here on earth using the progressive principles of liberalism—socialism, therapy, various appeals to science, etc. The last of Richard Rohr's ten commandments for a new orthodoxy declares, "Life in this world is more important than the afterlife."

The theology of the historic, biblical, and creedal gospel conflicts with the whole progressive project, which turns Christianity into a mere call for social reform. As 20th-century American Christian ethicist Richard Niebuhr once famously said about progressive theology: "A God without wrath brought men without sin into a kingdom without judgment through the ministrations of a Christ without a cross." I might add to Niebuhr's quote: "through a religion without a gospel."

Start with the sinfulness of humanity. The apostolic witness insists that the gospel is necessary because of the sinfulness of humanity. The Bible is clear that though humans were created good, sin has stained all of humanity. From cover to cover the Bible describes the sins of both Jew and Gentile and explains over and again that God is just in his punishing people for their sinfulness. This is explicitly affirmed by the whole Old Testament, by the whole New Testament, by the historic teachers and martyrs of the church, and by the great creeds and theology of the universal church. Some sins are more social in nature—the taking of bribes, the exploitation of the poor, unjust violence, the neglect of widows, and the like. Other sins are more personal in nature—adultery, homosexual activity, lying, cheating, stealing, and so forth. Above all of these sins lies the greatest sin of all: exchanging the true God for false gods made to look like us, which is idolatry.

We could list many of the Scriptures that demonstrate this non-negotiable starting point for the gospel—that we are all hopelessly lost in sin.

But we don't have to. In his letter to the Romans, the apostle Paul partially did it for us:

> [A]ll, both Jews and Greeks, are under sin, as it is written: "None is righteous, no, not one; no one understands; no one seeks for God. All have turned aside; together they have become worthless; no one does good, not even one." "Their throat is an open grave; they use their tongues to deceive." "The venom of asps is under their lips." "Their mouth is full of curses and bitterness." "Their feet are swift to shed blood; in their paths are ruin and misery, and the way of peace they have not known." "There is no fear of God before their eyes." (Rom. 3:9-18, citing multiple Old Testament texts)

One doesn't have to be a Calvinist to affirm the biblical teaching about original sin. Arminians have their version of original sin too.[56] Both Calvin and Arminius taught that all humans are guilty and have the proclivity to sin. And long before either Calvin or Arminius, the church knew that we humans gravitate toward sin. Augustine describes his own propensity to sin when he tells the story from his teenage years of stealing pears from his neighbor's yard. It wasn't the fruit he wanted; rather, it was the enjoyment of sin that he craved. And the more depraved he could appear before his buddies, the more perverse joy it gave him.[57]

Another of Richard Rohr's ten commandments is that we should stop worrying about sex. Rohr neglects the destructive nature of the sexual revolution, as most progressives do. And he also fails to understand how the sexual appetite can actually demonstrate the inherent sinfulness of humanity. With each exposure to pornography and illicit sex, a person requires increasingly perverse sexual expressions in order to find satisfaction. Child pornography is nothing other than fallen human nature allowed to continue unchecked. Seems reasonable to assume that child pornographers would be among those who "stopped worrying about sex." Though not explicitly stated, that's the result of this kind of thinking.

We can describe it in several ways, but the truth is that we sin because we love sin. And it is precisely this love of evil that contradicts the optimism of progressivism. Indeed, with the work of Augustine, by the 5th century, the Christian church had recognized that any view which presumed the general goodness of humans is not only wrong, it is heresy.

The 5th-century Pelagian controversy was exactly about this point. Though we aren't fully sure what all he said, the British monk Pelagius argued that we humans have the capacity to live good lives on our own. Many Brits followed his optimism before the rest of the church responded by pointing out that both Scripture and experience render the teachings of Pelagius a heresy—that is, a different gospel. The optimism that liberalism brings to Christianity is unsupported by the apostolic witness; it is another gospel.[58] It shares common assumptions with Pelagianism. But it is wrong. We are simply incapable of perfecting ourselves.[59]

And this assessment of sinful humanity actually aligns with our experience. Who among us, when we finally admit the truth, couldn't agree with Paul's evaluation of his own sinful will: "I do not understand my own actions. For I do not do what I want, but I do the very thing I hate …. For I have the desire to do what is right, but not the ability to carry it out. For I do not do the good I want, but the evil I do not want is what I keep on doing …. Wretched man that I am!" (Rom. 7:15-24). Proof of our sinful nature is all around us and offers a driving concern for any variety of human endeavors: politics, jurisprudence, psychology, sociology, and more. As G. K. Chesterton once quipped, "Original sin is the only part of Christian theology which can really be proved."

Progressives are often naïve or outright dishonest about evil, downplaying its reality or simply denying its existence. White North American elites can afford to deny evil in the world because, as I mentioned above, most have never really experienced great injustice, oppression, persecution, or national calamity. But the truth is that evil has run rampant across history. Most humans know this because most humans have experienced it—and this is why most humans could never afford the luxury of theological liberalism. This is why I say that progressivism is the religion of upper class, white Western people.

Persecuted minorities in Nigeria, Pakistan, or Tibet could never make sense of theological liberalism. Nor could the world's hundreds of millions who live on the edges of survival. Nor, for that matter, could any culture that is not in the process of renouncing orthodox Christianity. Progressivism is, as I've suggested, a halfway house for restless elites who are leaving the faith and headed for unbelief in general. The victims of the evils of Stalin, Hitler, Mao, Pol Pot, and Castro were not just suffering from low self-esteem—they suffered real, horrible evil. Aleksandr Solzhenitsyn, who started out with utopic visions of social justice before he nearly starved to death in socialist gulags, captures it well: "[T]he line dividing good and evil cuts through the heart of every human being."[60]

And so the death of Jesus was required as an atonement for human sin. Jesus died a martyr, and there is a sense in which his death was a tragedy—insofar as human sin put him on the cross. But ultimately, the death of Jesus is about God's grace-filled plan to save humans by taking upon himself in the person of Jesus Christ our unholiness and the penalty for our sins so that we could be restored to fellowship with him. His *atonement*.

The Bible explains the death of Jesus as something done *for us*. The scriptural evidence is overwhelming:

- "But he was wounded for our transgressions; he was crushed for our iniquities; upon him was the chastisement that brought us peace, and with his stripes we are healed" (Isaiah 53:5).
- "He is the propitiation for our sins, and not for ours only but also for the sins of the whole world" (1 John 2:2).
- "I am the good shepherd. The good shepherd lays down his life for the sheep" (John 10:11).
- "And he took a cup, and when he had given thanks he gave it to them, saying, 'Drink of it, all of you, for this is my blood of the covenant, which is poured out for many for the forgiveness of sins'" (Matthew 26:27-28).
- "For even the Son of Man came not to be served but to serve, and to give his life as a ransom for many" (Mark 10:45).
- "God shows his love for us in that while we were still sinners, Christ died for us .... For if while we were enemies we were reconciled to God by the death of his Son, much more, now that we are reconciled, shall we be saved by his life" (Romans 5:8-10).
- "In this is love, not that we have loved God but that he loved us and sent his Son to be the propitiation for our sins" (1 John 4:10).

And the list goes on. Now, it's true that there are various theories for how atonement works, but every theory that wants to be Christian includes some version of Christ dying so that our sins might be forgiven.[61] As the Niceno-Constantinopolitan Creed succinctly puts it, "… one Lord Jesus Christ …. Who *for us men*, and *for our salvation*, came down and was incarnate and … was crucified for us under Pontius Pilate." Or, as the Westminster Confession puts it, "Christ, by his obedience and death, did fully discharge the debt of all those that are thus justified, and did make a proper, real, and full satisfaction to his Father's justice in their behalf."[62]

Progressives don't like atonement, in part because they don't like the concept of sin and judgment. But atonement theory is critical to the Christian faith because it preserves both God's justice and his mercy. Indeed, without the atonement, God would be an unjust God, for it would mean that God is okay with the many crimes we have committed against one another. It would mean that God is good with a world where there is massive abuse, destruction, ethnic cleansing, racism, lying, stealing, hoarding, insulting, maiming, raping, and killing.

There is no justice where evil is ignored or denied. Wrongs must be borne by somebody: the one who commits them, the one against whom they are committed, or the world at large. Justice demands that those who commit wrongs bear the responsibility. The God of the Christian faith is not unjust—he will hold creation responsible for the evil it commits. And to suggest, as some progressives do, that God's punishment for our sins comes to us only in this life—when we feel shame or guilt or pain for what we've done—is a luxury opinion of the elite. The rest of the world knows better. Emmett Till was lynched in Mississippi in 1955 at the age of fourteen. To suggest that the only punishment the murderers of young innocents like Till will face is low self-esteem ridicules justice. We deserve the punishment our sins have earned. And God is going to provide it. As Jesus promised (in red letters!), "And will not God bring about justice for his chosen ones, who cry out to him day and night? Will he keep putting them off? I tell you, he will see that they get justice, and quickly" (Luke 18:7-8).

Progressives will find a way to deny atonement because they don't want to believe that we are sinners who will be punished by a just God. But they also avoid doctrines about atonement because they don't like the idea of Jesus as divine.[63] Remember that progressives have leaned Unitarian for nearly two hundred years; to declare Jesus divine necessarily requires the affirmation of the rightness of the Christian religion above all other religions. It undermines universalism, a doctrine many progressives want to be true.[64]

Bottom line is that the doctrine of atonement only works if Jesus is divine. If Jesus were a mere human, the doctrine of atonement would be tantamount to criminal, for it would imply that God punished the man Jesus for the sins of others. Progressives thus reveal their disbelief in the deity of Jesus when they declare the doctrine of atonement to be "cosmic child abuse."[65] If Jesus is divine, then God didn't punish one man for another man's sins. Rather, as the Bible teaches, Jesus is "God among us" (Emmanuel); Jesus himself *is* God, who takes upon *himself* the sins of the world.

Several years ago, I had the privilege of sharing dinner with Annie Lobert.[66] Annie grew up in a family of six in Minnesota, and though her mom took the children to church, she remembers a father who was harsh, frightening, and, at times, abusive. At some point in her teen life, Annie began to rebel. Filled with insecurities, suffering from bulimia, and desperately needing to be loved, Annie hung out with any crowd that would offer her what felt like acceptance.

Annie was physically attractive, and having been groomed by an American culture that emphasizes glitter, glitz, romance, fashion, and power, she soon found herself attracted to a group of friends who were making enormous amounts of money. As it turned out, her wealthy friends were making money through prostitution. Soon, Annie began to prostitute herself.

At first, the money and power were intoxicating. Even though she knew that prostitution was not love, Annie felt a degree of love from her pimp and even from some of her johns. More than this, however, Annie found her alter ego in prostitution—a strong, sophisticated, and well-liked woman. In the words of decadent America, Annie found her "authentic self" in prostitution. She adopted the name of her favorite TV personality, Fallon, from the TV show *Dynasty*. When she moved to Las Vegas, she was able to charge anywhere from $500 to $1,000 per client.

But trouble soon began. Her boyfriend, it turned out, was a violent pimp. Though he spoiled her at times, he also began to control her. He decided when and where she could go. He decided what she could do and who she would be. He required her to see as many as ten clients per night.

He would not permit her to contact her family. He often raped her, and to reinforce his authority over her, he often beat her, at times severely enough to threaten her very life. He was the absolute master, and she was the slave. The profession she had chosen as an emotional refuge turned out to be a torture chamber. Annie was lost. No fewer than thirteen of her prostitute friends ended up either dead or permanently missing.

After several years of hell, Annie decided she had to get away from her pimp. She had stashed away cash, and through a series of events, found herself on the run. Her story was not smooth, nor was her escape from the bondage of sin. But it began when she found a Bible in a hotel room and began to read about grace and forgiveness from the very Son of God. Though she continued to fall, she started moving toward Christ.

Finally, after cancer, the loss of a dear friend, and a drug addiction, Annie was on the edge of death. She took a hit of cocaine and passed out. While she was unconscious, Annie had a dream about her own funeral. She describes it:

> The scene was dark with a bright light spotlighting a coffin. As I walked toward the pine box, I saw me inside. Then I saw my family come up to the coffin, one by one, crying and shaking their heads. "What a waste," someone said. "She was an addicted prostitute. We never knew. What happened to our little girl?"[67]

Annie was being rushed to the hospital when she woke up. Tears rolled down her face as she realized that she needed salvation. Not knowing if she would live or die, Annie began to pray to Jesus—to the Jesus she had read of in the Bible: "Please give me another chance! Please forgive me for all that I have done. I don't want to die!"

Annie should have died that day, as the level of drugs in her bloodstream was lethal. But she didn't. Instead, she lived, and she gave her life to Jesus. She was done with the prostitution. She was done with the drugs. She was done with the painkillers, the smoking, the pain, the shame, and the disaster that was her life. The Jesus of Scripture saved her, and Annie rose to become a new person: "No more going back. No more staying up all night for days on end getting high. No more desperate thoughts of running away from myself and hiding from the cruel world. No more night-mares of wearing a mask, pretending everything had turned out perfectly. Fallon died that night. I knew that my old life was now over, and a new one was beginning! I was on my way to a beautiful place of redemption and promise. Hello, sweet Jesus, here I come."[68]

Annie was saved that night, and she has since given her life to sav-ing other women caught in the sex-trade industry. She has raised tons of money, founded a halfway house, and spoken all over the nation about the evils of prostitution. And everywhere she goes, she calls people to enter a relationship, not with a mere ethical system or social utopia but with a real Jesus—the Jesus of the Scriptures—who doesn't tell us what we want to hear about human goodness but, instead, rescues us from the reality of our brokenness.

Annie needed more than an ethical strategist, a social reformer, or a "good man." She needed more than a simple close look deep inside for the purpose of finding her true self. Annie needed grace, forgiveness, healing, and the salvation that only the Son of God himself can offer. Annie need-ed atonement, not just a social theory or self-affirmations. Annie needed holiness. Annie needed a God who loves her personally and offers her a personal relationship. And in Jesus, she found her atonement.

When Annie spoke at my church several years ago, I suggested that she not offer an "altar call," as her speaking engagement was more a school-type lecture. She said something back to me like "whatever." Then, she offered one of the clearest altar calls ever given at our church: "Even when I was that prostitute, he loved me. And he loves you. He loves you. He loves you. Come to him as you are, and he will set you free! And *that's* the truth."

In Jesus, God offers real forgiveness, real grace, and real salvation. That's because Jesus is God incarnate, who took upon himself flesh in or-der to save us. And so in the next chapter we turn to the deity of Jesus, the most non-negotiable element of the Christian faith.

Chapter 6

Jesus: Divine Son or Social Activist?

"Too hot! Too hot!"

These were the words of a nine-year-old girl—*the* nine-year-old girl. You know her, even if you don't know it.

She is Phan Thi Kim Phuc, and she is the napalm girl: the little girl running naked out of the Vietnamese village of Trang Bang after the temple where she had sought refuge was accidentally napalmed in 1972. The Pulitzer Prize-winning photograph taken of her by AP photographer Nick Ut is one of the world's most important photographs. You've seen it: on the front page of the *New York Times*, in history books, and throughout a thousand other sources. The picture helped end the Vietnam War.

The gelatin flames covered the back of her body, searing it at five thousand degrees Fahrenheit and causing damage you don't want to think about. After the picture, Kim passed out. But Mr. Ut did not just take her picture. He also had her taken to a hospital, but the medical staff there presumed she was dying so they placed her burned little body in the morgue. There was no way she could survive.

But she did survive. And though most are unaware of it, after fourteen months in the hospital and multiple surgeries, Kim was released from the hospital, where her nightmare continued. The war eventually destroyed her village and made her once middle class family destitute refugees. They were robbed, almost killed trying to escape the country, and eventually forced to live under the brutalities of the communist government. Then, war broke out between the Vietnamese and the Cambodians, and new horrors faced the beautiful people of Vietnam.

Kim was caught in all of this, bearing not only horrible scars but also unending pain from the burns. She managed to finish school and sought to enroll in medical school, determined to become like the doctors who had saved her life. But the Vietnamese government had other purposes for her. They removed her from school and forced her to do numerous propaganda interviews against the United States (whom she liked)—showing her burns as a testimony against American imperialists.

Inside, Kim was dying. She had no friends. Her beauty had been taken from her. People sometimes avoided her because of the extensive scars. She had not experienced a single moment of joy since that fateful morning in 1972 when the sky exploded in napalm. Her body was constantly racked with pain. Her government used her as a puppet. And her religion, Cao-Dai, had failed her.

CaoDai is a Vietnamese religion that, at least in Kim's experience, recognizes all religious paths as leading to God. It is a universalist religion not unlike American liberalism in its emphasis on doing good works instead of having a personal relationship with a loving God. But when Kim needed her religion the most, it could not offer her peace or comfort, or a reason to live. Kim needed a God who would live inside of her, transform her, and save her. Above all, Kim needed a God who would love her and develop a relationship with her. Her civic religion of good works and ritual could offer her nothing.

And so sitting in a library in 1982, ten years after her village was napalmed, Kim considered suicide.

At the end of her rope, Kim rummaged through the religious section of the library and stumbled on the New Testament. She began reading, and soon, she was engrossed in the Bible, especially the Gospel of John. Who is this Jesus? John's Gospel states that Jesus doesn't just bring us an ethical system but also that Jesus offers us a personal relationship with God through him—along with life, joy, and salvation. She was enthralled with Jesus, whose name had only been a vague concept before.

Within a few days, Kim sought out a church to find out more about this Jesus. Wandering into the first church she could find, Kim began to hear about Jesus, the Son of God. She began to hear about his personal love for her—whom nobody seemed to love. Her pastor told her that she doesn't have to earn God's love in order to receive his grace. She even learned that this God, who came to earth through Jesus Christ, wanted Kim to be his bride. She knew that in her old religion she had tried everything and it hadn't worked. In the way of Jesus, she learned, it was never going to be about trying harder; it was going to be about trusting and loving the Son of God. It was going to be about the grace God would give her in Jesus alone. It would be a personal relationship that would change everything for her.

After several months of attending a church, hearing Jesus preached, praying, and studying Scripture, Kim was ready. She had felt worthless and unloved for years. In Jesus, she would find peace, joy, abundance, and true life.

So in 1982, Kim Phuc, the napalm girl, gave her life to Jesus—not to a progressive ideology, a social program, or a political slogan—all of which her communist government was *already* offering. None of these had done anything to resolve her inner pain. Instead, Kim gave her life to the Son of God personally. And in him, she found life: "I would surrender one thousand hearts to this Jesus, had I that many hearts to give," she explained.[69]

Kim eventually escaped from communist Vietnam to Canada, where she lives as a faithful disciple of Jesus, married with two sons and grandchildren, and has more joy and love than she can describe.

Today, Kim oversees the Kim Phuc Foundation, which is an international organization that helps child victims of war. She is actively involved in social justice but not as a replacement for her salvation. Rather, her foundation flows out of her personal salvation and the gospel of Jesus that saved her. Personal faith in Jesus as the divine Son of God changed Kim's heart and saved her soul. He is the source of peace. He is the source of joy. He is the source of life. And because of what he did for Kim, she shares peace with the rest of the world.

I spent much of the day with Kim Phuc, the napalm girl, some time back; I have never been with a person who has more joy than Kim. As we spoke of the amazing journey God had led her through, Kim emphasized to me that it was her personal relationship with the divine Jesus that had saved her, her husband, her sons, her parents, and others from her village. All of them were accustomed to social activism—they had, after all, lived under communist government where politics *is* the national religion. She didn't need activism. She needed the Son of God. And the story of Jesus is not, ultimately, a story of activism, good works, and ritual; the story of Jesus is the story of how God became human to save everyone who accepts his kingship.

Jesus the Divine

Scripture is filled with references to Jesus' divinity. Even if we didn't have the Nicene or Chalcedonian Creeds stating the orthodox view on this point, Scripture is still sufficiently clear here. Every time Scripture calls Jesus "the Son of God," it's making a divine claim, for this is what the term meant in Greek. Herakles was "son of a god." Various Semitic and Hellenistic kings referred to themselves as "the son of a god." The Caesars took to calling themselves "sons of god." Such titles did not simply mean "my daddy is a god." Rather, one used the title "son of God" to claim actual divine status.

John explains it to us: "This was why the Jews were seeking all the more to kill him, because not only was he breaking the Sabbath, but he was even calling God his own father, making himself equal with God" (John 5:18). Jesus was not killed as a mere human martyr for social causes. He was killed as part of a divine plan: he came as God among us to take upon himself the price of our sins.

Thus, even though the Scriptures don't work out all the implications for calling Jesus God, there are biblical texts that make it clear that both Jesus and the first Christians understood Jesus to be divine. Consider a few:

- "For to us a child is born, to us a son is given; and the government shall be upon his shoulder, and his name shall be called Wonderful Counselor, Mighty God, Everlasting Father, Prince of Peace" (Isaiah 9:6).
- "Jesus said to them, 'Truly, truly, I say to you, before Abraham was, I am'" (John 8:58).

- "It is not for a good work that we are going to stone you but for blasphemy, because you, being a man, make yourself God" (John 10:33).
- "In the beginning was the Word, and the Word was with God, and the Word was God .... And the Word became flesh and dwelt among us ..." (John 1:1, 14).
- "Pay careful attention to yourselves and to all the flock, in which the Holy Spirit has made you overseers, to care for the church of God, which he obtained with his own blood" (Acts 20:28).
- "[The Son] is the radiance of the glory of God and the exact imprint of his nature, and he upholds the universe by the word of his power. After making purification for sins, he sat down at the right hand of the Majesty on high .... [O]f the Son he says, 'Your throne, O God, is forever and ever, the scepter of uprightness is the scepter of your kingdom.' And, 'You, Lord, laid the foundation of the earth in the beginning, and the heavens are the work of your hands ...'" (Hebrews 1:3-10).
- "He is the image of the invisible God, the firstborn of all creation. For by him all things were created, in heaven and on earth, visible and invisible, whether thrones or dominions or rulers or authorities—all things were created through him and for him. And he is before all things, and in him all things hold together" (Colossians 1:15-17).
- "Simeon Peter, a servant and apostle of Jesus Christ, to those who have obtained a faith of equal standing with ours by the righteousness of our God and Savior Jesus Christ ..." (2 Peter 1:1).
- "For the grace of God has appeared, bringing salvation for all people, training us to renounce ungodliness and worldly passions, and to live self-controlled, upright, and godly lives in the present age, waiting for our blessed hope, the appearing of the glory of our great God and Savior Jesus Christ ..." (Titus 2:11-13).
- "To them [the Jews] belong the patriarchs, and from their race, according to the flesh, is the Christ who is God over all, blessed forever. Amen" (Romans 9:5).

The doctrine of the divinity of Jesus is non-negotiable for the Christian faith. To deny that Jesus is divine is to deny that he is the Son of God. In the apostolic days, the heresy of Gnosticism wrestled with the question but from a different angle. Gnostics believed that Jesus was divine, but they could not accept that God had come in flesh so they came up with various theories about how God only *seemed* to be human. John the apostle calls them anti-Christs (e.g., 1 John 2:18, 22). Liberals are the modern-day equivalents of the Gnostics—they, too, cannot accept that God would become flesh in the person of Jesus. But unlike Gnostics, they do not suggest that Jesus only appeared to be *human*. Rather, they suggest that Jesus only appeared to be *God*. Both are heresies. Both must be fully repudiated by Christians.

It took several hundred years of debate for the church to sort out how God can exist in three persons and how Jesus can be both human and divine. But when the church finally developed their formulas (expressed at Nicaea and Chalcedon and presumed in virtually every creed since), they were able to summarize Scripture in simple sentences. Their summaries account for the apostolic witness given us in Scripture: God is one essence in three persons; the Son is fully human and fully divine. Nothing is as fundamental to Christianity as these truths. And so when progressives recite the Nicene Creed (which many of their churches and schools require them to do), some are being deceitful. And when they practice their sacraments, they sometimes empty the sacraments of all their significance. What good is communion or baptism or unction without a Triune God and a Divine Son?

Jesus is both fully human and fully divine. This makes him more than a teacher of a new way. It makes him the Way itself—and the *only* way, at that. He himself says so (in red letters): "I am the way, and the truth, and the life. No one comes to the Father except through me .... Whoever has seen me has seen the Father" (John 14:6, 9). When we believe in Jesus and are justified by his blood, he personally brings God into our hearts. Paul exhorts us, "See to it that no one takes you captive by philosophy and empty deceit, according to human tradition, according to the elemental spirits of the world, and not according to Christ. For in him the whole fullness of deity dwells bodily, and you have been filled in him, who is the head of all rule and authority" (Col. 2:8-10).

Because Jesus is divine, his death is nothing less than God personally taking on our sins and suffering our penalty upon the cross. God does this because of his immense love for us. He doesn't want us to suffer. He wants us to live right and holy lives. And so, to preserve his justice but be consistent with his love, God came among us in the person of Jesus, took our guilt and unholiness upon himself, and paid our price. That's the gospel. It is the *only* gospel worth preaching.

I recently read about a Special Forces veteran in North Carolina who was struggling with major bouts of PTSD (Post-Traumatic Stress Disorder). He had been awarded three purple hearts, had been in battle multiple times, had been awarded multiple accolades, and had tragically seen the lives of some of his friends taken. Upon returning home, he fought the demons of substance abuse, finding himself in veterans court two dozen times. The article I read was written after he had confessed to the judge that he had cheated on his last urine test.[70]

The judge had a challenge on his hands. On the one hand, he could not simply ignore the vet's crime. To do so would be unjust: Do we really want judges who disregard the law whenever they are so moved? On the other hand, the judge was also a veteran and he was worried that a night in jail could push the vet to suicide. So judge Lou Olivera did a fascinating thing. He sentenced the vet to a night in jail—to be a just judge. But then, Olivera personally joined him in jail, staying up with him all night and talking to him like a father to a son and encouraging him. I don't know Olivera, but I bet I'd like him. He found a way to be both just and merciful.

This is a small model of the real gospel. We humans are guilty of sin and crimes, but God loves us so much that he found a way to personally enter into our world and take our punishment upon himself. This is grace—that God loves us enough to rescue us from our sin. The progressive message often implies that God is so uninterested in us that he would leave us in our sins—that there is no price to pay for sin. For progressives, grace can sometimes devolve into mere indulgence—the progressive God can easily become a God who allows people to commit atrocities against one another without penalty. But such a message can only be afforded by those who have lived lives of sufficient privilege to have never really suffered grave injustice.

The real gospel is the story of what God in Jesus did for us. His life taught us how we are to live, but his death offered us forgiveness for our failure to live this way. This makes the cross central to the story of Jesus. And this explains why all four New Testament Gospels point us forward to the cross. It also explains why, after the resurrection, even those who lived with Jesus and heard him speak often of the kingdom of God continued to focus on the cross and resurrection. It's striking that, after the cross, the apostles and prophets hardly speak of the life of Jesus at all. Rather, they speak of his atoning death and ongoing ministry in the church. Of course, this makes sense, for the ministry of Jesus only matters if he is the divine Son who died for our sins. Without the atoning cross, the story of Jesus would be just another sad story of a good man killed by his oppressors. When progressives stop their story of Jesus before the cross, they rob the story of its power. It's like reading a biography of Abraham Lincoln that doesn't include his presidency. The only reason we care about Lincoln is because he became President. And the only reason we would care about Jesus is because he is the Son of God who died, was raised, and is now King of kings.

The Resurrection of Jesus

Orthodox, biblical, historic Christianity does not stop at the death of Jesus. It goes straight from Jesus' death to his resurrection—which is the flip side of the same redemptive coin. In the death of Jesus, we get our sins forgiven, and in the resurrection of Jesus, we get a new life.

Progressives often struggle with the resurrection as well as with the cross, but for different reasons. Typically, progressives push back against the atoning death of Jesus, as we have seen, because they're skeptical about the sinfulness of humanity, the justice of God, or the divinity of Christ. But the pushback from progressives against the resurrection has to do with their scientific metanarrative about the universe. Progressives are dead serious about accepting the ideology of science. By this, I don't mean progressives pay too much respect to science; it seems to me that science has earned its respect. What I'm talking about is not science *per se* but science as ideology; that is, physicalism—the belief that physical particles are the ultimate explanation for everything. Since progressivism is largely a civic religion shaped by cultural expectations, respectability is crucial for progressives. And academic Americans frequently presume the myth of physicalism. To suggest that the miracles of the Bible actually happened violates the principles of physicalism, and therefore costs progressives respect in the eyes of physicalists.

But we should remember that physicalism is not science; rather, it is ideology. Even science knows that particles cannot account for the vast entity that is our cosmos; nor can it account for the broad range of experiences we humans have. Many progressives are beholden to physicalism (wrongly confused with "science"), and for this reason they simply cannot accept biblical claims about miracles. And so they turn the resurrection into poetry, metaphor, or myth—treating one of the most fundamental doctrines of Christianity as though it were a grade school Valentine's Day card.

Mike McHargue (aka "Science Mike" of the Liturgists) explains that he doesn't know if Jesus really was raised from the dead. Beholden to physicalism, McHargue then explains that it doesn't matter anyway: "You can be skeptical about the Resurrection of Jesus and still have an encounter with Jesus that's life-changing .... Jesus lives in my anterior cingulate cortex, the seat of compassion."[71] McHargue is simply repeating, in cool language, the old beliefs of mainline Protestant Liberalism. The Anglican Ambassador to the Vatican John Shepherd has come under fire for saying years ago that Christians should be "set free" from the idea that the resurrection was a physical event. Neither McHargue nor Shepherd seem aware that the apostle Paul explains that if Jesus were not literally raised from the dead, the Christian faith would be utterly irrelevant (1 Cor. 15:14).

The resurrection constitutes the core of the earliest preaching of the gospel, and it constitutes the very reason Christianity has survived for two thousand years. Had Jesus' death been the end of his story, you can be sure that nobody would have ever heard from his followers again. There would be no record of Jesus; he would've been just one more statistic from the Roman world of brutality. Because Jesus was raised from the dead, appeared to his followers, then arose into heaven to assume a seat next to the Father, the Christian religion exploded onto the world stage to become the world's largest religion. Missionary scholar Herbert Kane captures the significance:

Although his untimely death at the age of 33 sent his disciples into confusion, His resurrection on the third day revived their Messianic hope, rejuvenated their flagging spirits, and sent them out to win the world. Their task was formidable. Their chances of success? Almost nil. They had no central organization, no financial resources, no influential friends, no political machine. Arrayed against them was the ecclesiastical power of the Sanhedrin, the political and military power of the Roman Empire, and the religious fanaticism of the Jews. Moreover, their leader, whose life and teachings were to constitute their message was unknown outside his small circle of friends. He had written no books, erected no monuments, endowed no institutions. The task looked hopeless.[72]

Through the resurrection of Jesus, millions would come to faith in Christ—and they would change the world. This explains why Jesus himself spoke of his resurrection, why the early church preached it, and why any effort to be Christian must embrace it. Let these Scriptures sink in:

- *Jesus predicted it:* "See, we are going up to Jerusalem. And the Son of Man will be delivered over to the chief priests and scribes, and they will condemn him to death and deliver him over to the Gentiles to be mocked and flogged and crucified, and he will be raised on the third day" (Matthew 20:18-19).
- *The early church preached it:* "For I delivered to you as of first importance what I also received: that Christ died for our sins in accordance with the Scriptures, that he was buried, that he was raised on the third day in accordance with Scripture, and that he appeared to Cephas, then to the Twelve. Then he appeared to more than five hundred brothers at one time, most of whom are still alive, though some have fallen asleep. Then he appeared to James, then to all the apostles. Last of all, as to one untimely born, he appeared also to me" (1 Corinthians 15:3-8).
- *And anyone who wants to be Christian will embrace it:* "For if the dead are not raised, not even Christ has been raised. And if

Christ has not been raised, your faith is futile and you are still in your sins. Then those also who have fallen asleep in Christ have perished. If in this life only we have hoped in Christ, we are of all people most to be pitied" (1 Corinthians 15:16-19).

If you're a member of a local church ministry or body, I encourage you to ask your pastor or leader (or maybe university professor) if they believe that Jesus was literally raised from the dead. You have a right to know what your leadership actually believes. Unfortunately, occasionally leaders who have used the language of resurrection in public have whispered to me in private that they believe the resurrection is more of metaphor than an actual historical event.

The resurrection of Jesus from the dead is a non-negotiable for the Christian faith. And not as a metaphor or mere poetry. As history. For the Christian religion is not grounded in ideology, psychology, or philosophy. It's rooted in historical fact: *God in Christ became human, died to save humans, and literally rose from the dead to give life to humanity.*

And now, Christ lives as both Savior and Lord over all creation, and he will return to raise humans from the dead to judge them and to establish a new heaven and earth.

The Lordship of Jesus

Progressives often challenge the atoning death of Jesus and doubt the resurrection. Consistent with progressivism's tendency to rewrite the gospel, progressivism sometimes treats the current Lordship of Jesus and his ultimate return with skepticism. Some progressives simply dismiss these essential and life-giving truths.

From the Bible and historical Christianity, to the Fathers of the church, and to the creeds, orthodox Christian doctrine makes it perfectly clear that Jesus now sits at the right hand of God's throne and demands our loyalty to *him*—not mere loyalty to principles of justice or kindness or "authenticity." If you think about it, this is the entire call of the New Testament: that we are to put our faith in Christ and submit to his Lordship.

As Peter announces right after the resurrection: "Let all the house of Israel therefore know for certain that God has made him both Lord and

Christ, this Jesus whom you crucified" (Acts 2:36). The Scripture calls us not to simply be nice to each other, to tweet celebrity causes, or to protest disfavored public policies. Rather, the Scripture calls for us to believe *personally* that Jesus is both Lord and Savior and to swear allegiance to him as King.[73]

Tragically, much of progressivism tends to stop the Jesus story short of his coronation as king—believing that the most important part of Jesus' story is his earthly ministry—his parables, his feeding of the hungry, or his healing of the sick. The so-called "Red Letter Christians" may emphasize the life of Jesus over his cross, but the early church knew better. The early church knew that the coronation of Christ is the peak of the gospel; it is what transforms us. The good works Jesus practiced are important, but they are only important if Jesus is now the King of kings who demands personal faith and loyalty to him. If you want to know what King Jesus demands of his followers, you must complete his story by reading the Book of Acts, the epistles, and the Book of Revelation. The rest of the New Testament offers divine interpretation and application of Jesus' ministry. And it's precisely these parts of the New Testament that progressives tend to neglect.

For progressives, the lordship of Jesus is problematic because it makes personal demands of people—demands that separate Christians from non-Christians. But isn't this exactly what Jesus came to do? In red letters, Matthew records Jesus' words, "Do not think that I have come to bring peace to the earth. I have not come to bring peace, but a sword. For I have come to set a man against his father, and a daughter against her mother, and a daughter-in-law against her mother-in-law" (Matt. 10:34-35). Jesus didn't come to declare that everybody wins. And Jesus did not come to be inclusive of everyone *as is*. Rather, he came to call us into holiness and life—and out of unholiness and death. He came to include everyone *who is willing to repent*. Jesus was and continues to be divisive. Anyone who makes the kind of claims on other people's lives that he made is going to be divisive. He *should* be divisive.

I discuss below more about the specific demands Jesus places on our lives, but suffice it to say here that Jesus' Lordship calls all of us to live repentant lives: "Do you think that these Galileans were worse sinners than all the other Galileans, because they suffered in this way? No, I tell you;

but unless you repent, you will all likewise perish" (Luke 13:2-3). It's worth remembering that the very first word of the gospel is the word "repent" (Matt. 4:17).

Jesus is Lord over all creation, ruling from the right hand of the throne of God the Father. Let's look at more of what his Lordship means and brings to us as his heirs (though far from an exhaustive list):

- Jesus came to earth to become King (John 18:37).
- Jesus has been given "dominion and glory and a kingdom, that all people, nations, and languages should serve him" and "his dominion is an everlasting dominion, which shall not pass away, and his kingdom one that shall not be destroyed" (Daniel 7:13-14).
- Jesus allows others to worship him as God (Matthew 2:11; 14:33; 28:9; John 21:27-28; Revelation 1:17).
- It is Jesus—and only Jesus—who makes us right with God (Romans 1-5).
- We enter into that relationship through faith sealed by baptism into Jesus (Romans 6:1-4).
- Jesus reigns in his church as Lord. He baptizes us with his Holy Spirit (1 Corinthians 12:13); Jesus completes us as disciples (Colossians 2:10).
- Jesus intercedes for us (Romans 8:34).
- Jesus is our head (Colossians 1:18; 1 Corinthians 11:3).
- Jesus connects us to the love of God (Romans 8:36-37).

Indeed, the Lordship of Jesus is so fundamental to his ongoing work that Paul's favorite term for discipleship is being "in Christ." So for those in Christ, "There is one God, the Father, from whom are all things and for whom we exist, and one Lord, Jesus Christ, through whom are all things and through whom we exist" (1 Cor. 8:5-6).

None of this is possible if we stop the story of Jesus at his earthly ministry. So we say it again: the earthly ministry of Jesus only matters because he is now reigning as Lord of lords and King of kings. The rest of the story and the part that matters most to us—is the ongoing Lordship of Jesus that began with his resurrection and will continue forever.

John's vision of Christ as victor puts the exclamation point on this:

> Then I saw heaven opened, and behold, a white horse!
> The one sitting on it is called Faithful and True, and in
> righteousness he judges and makes war. His eyes are like
> a flame of fire, and on his head are many diadems, and he
> has a name written that no one knows but himself. He is
> clothed in a robe dipped in blood, and the name by which
> he is called is The Word of God. And the armies of heaven,
> arrayed in fine linen, white and pure, were following him
> on white horses. From his mouth comes a sharp sword
> with which to strike down the nations, and he will rule
> them with a rod of iron. He will tread the winepress of
> the fury of the wrath of God the Almighty. On his robe
> and on his thigh he has a name written, King of kings and
> Lord of lords. (Rev. 19:11-16)

Christ's work is far, far more than his earthly ministry, which is overshadowed by his ongoing ministry of Kingship.

Matthew Bates's work in his excellent book *Salvation by Allegiance* is helpful here. Bates meticulously establishes that there is only one gospel, which is "the transformative story of how Jesus, who pre-existed as Son of God, came to be enthroned as the universal king."[74] Bates demonstrates that there are eight elements in the gospel. Jesus the king:

1. Pre-existed with the Father,
2. Took on human flesh, fulfilling God's promises to David,
3. Died for sins in accordance with Scripture,
4. Was buried,
5. Was raised on the third day in accordance with the Scriptures,
6. Appeared to many,
7. *Is seated at the right hand of God as Lord*, and
8. Will come again as judge.[75]

The highpoint of the gospel, Bates demonstrates, is not element two, as progressives argue. Jesus did not come merely to be a role model. Neither is the high point element three, as some evangelicals preach. Jesus didn't merely come to give us forgiveness of sins. Rather, the peak of the gospel is element seven: Jesus is now reigning as Lord of creation. If we don't look beyond points two or three, we miss the full gospel and rob those we teach of what they most desperately need—a King and Lord who will both save *and* rule over them. Jesus is now King; he is not just a role model.

The Final Return of Jesus

We end this chapter focusing on the culmination of Jesus' Lordship—his return and judgment upon creation. Scripture clearly tells us that those who have put their trust in him will be raised up to a new life in a new Jerusalem in a new heaven and earth. And those who have refused to trust Christ will be cast into a place Jesus calls "hell."

We learn about his returning judgment through Jesus himself who speaks about it often. Let's look at some examples:

- In his lament over Jerusalem, Jesus declares that he will return after his death in the clouds with power and great glory, and that all will see him as he gathers his elect from the four corners of the earth and as the evil are punished (Matthew 24:30-51).
- Later, Jesus describes the day of judgment as a separation of sheep and goats (Matthew 25:31ff).
- Explaining his death, Jesus tells the apostles that he is actually going to prepare a place for them, then promises that he will return to take them there (John 14:1-3).
- He is specific about the coming judgment: "An hour is coming when all who are in the tombs will hear his voice and come out, those who have done good to the resurrection of life, and those who have done evil to the resurrection of judgment" (John 5:28-29).
- And after the resurrection, Jesus ascends into heaven, and two angels announce to the disciples that Jesus will return just as he has ascended (Acts 1:11).

The Second Coming with its resurrection of the dead is the hope of Christians because we cannot fix this broken world. As the apostle Paul says, this world groans under the weight of sin (Rom. 8:22-23). But Christ loves us enough to give us a new world. So the coming judgment of Jesus is good news for his followers. It means that the suffering, pain, failure, and shame we endure in this life will be redeemed in the next.

In Revelation, John describes this new world as looking a whole lot like, but far exceeding, the original paradise of the Garden of Eden—complete with the river of life, streets of gold, gates of pearl, and the very presence of God himself (Rev. 21-22). How much of John's description of the New Jerusalem is to be taken as representative language where ordinary language simply cannot communicate I don't know. But I do know that dismissing the prophecy that a new creation is coming is a slap in the face to the Christian faith. As early as Isaiah the prophet, God was promising a new creation (Isa. 65:17), and the New Testament confirms that promise (2 Pet. 3:13). Those who have put their faith in Jesus will one day hear him say, "Enter into the joy of your master" (Matt. 25:23).

What about hell, though?

If there is any doctrine that progressives find repugnant, it's the biblical doctrine of hell. Brian McLaren speaks for progressives when he says that Jesus' teaching on hell is false advertising: it negates the goodness of God. God is good, McLaren insists, and he's right about that. But, he claims, this means that God cannot punish evildoers as Jesus taught:

> [I]n an ironic way, the doctrine of hell basically says [of the goodness of God], no, that's not really true. That in the end, God gets His way through coercion and violence and intimidation and domination, just like every other kingdom does. The cross isn't the center then. The cross is almost a distraction and false advertising for God.[76]

McLaren and other progressives contend that there simply is no way that a loving God could banish people to hell. But it's important to understand that much of what progressives protest is the vision of hell painted by the medievalists—by Dante and Bosch—not the picture of hell in the Bible. The Scriptures describe hell in horrific ways but in ways that are clearly symbolic of a trash pile. Indeed, the very term "hell" is translated from a Greek (and, before that, Hebrew) term referring to the trash pile outside of Jerusalem—characterized by literal fire and maggots. The metaphor of hell is that of a burning trash pile; actual hell may be something altogether different.

In any case, the biblical teaching about hell is actually good news because it declares that in the new creation, those who have committed unrepentant crimes against others, against creation, and against God will have no place. They will be in the city's forgotten trash heap. This means that those who have struggled to follow Jesus, who have loved God, who have dealt with pain faithfully, who have suffered in hope, and who have been persecuted because of their faith will find themselves in a new place, where the tears, pains, and sufferings of the past are banished, where evil no longer exists, and where their tormenters are not allowed.

In the new creation, all things will be made new.

Hell is also good news because it reassures us that God is a just God. As we've already talked about, North American aristocrats can downplay God's justice because they have always been on the winning side of justice. It's why many elites promote indulgence rather than justice—justice works to their advantage, so they have the luxury of indulgence. However, most of the world hasn't enjoyed justice and is longing to know that God is just. Where justice has not been offered to the masses—where most of the masses have endured neglect, abuse, oppression, and scorn—the truth of hell is a promise in this life that the God they worship and serve will one day right all wrongs in the new world.

But hell is also, in a strange way, good news for those who don't want God. Ultimately, both heaven and hell turn out to be God giving you what you want. Those in the new creation longed for a life with God, and they now receive it. Those in hell longed for a life without God, and in hell, they receive it. Those in hell wanted a world with no moral boundaries. In hell, they get one. At its simplest definition, hell is eternity without God. Anyone who goes to hell goes there because they wanted a life without God. Maggots are in the trash because that's where they want to be. Nobody is forced to go there. In a similar way, people go to a godless hell because they want a godless life. Nobody is forced to go there.

This explains why Jesus speaks about hell more than any other person in the New Testament.[77] As the author of love, Jesus understands that people go to hell because they want to. And he gives them what they want. Is hell punishment? Most certainly. But life without God on earth is hell too. Why shouldn't those who choose hell here receive it in the hereafter also?

Granted, I'm not arguing that the orthodox, biblical message makes perfect sense to secular North Americans. I can't say that it does. What I can say is that *hardly anything* in orthodox Christianity makes sense in secular America. But when we choose to follow Jesus, we choose to accept what he teaches (or we never really chose him in the first place). And we learn to understand through obedience. When we embrace his teachings and obey them, they unfold before us with power, truth, and beauty. They become life. I mean this literally—the more we follow the Jesus of Scripture, the more we understand him, even his tough doctrines, the more we experience true life. Paul's comment about the Torah is true about the whole Bible: "We know that the Torah is spiritual; the problem is that I'm a slave to sin" (Rom. 7:14, my translation).

And so with the apostle Paul, we relish in the cross, finding great joy in the atonement. Our own struggles with sin are disclosed by the truth and light of Scripture, helping us understand ourselves and showing us the path to freedom. We submit not only to the red letters of the Synoptics but also to the ongoing work of the King of kings and Lord of lords in all the Bible. We understand that the entire New Testament witnesses the resurrected and crowned King Jesus, who is the Christ, the Lord, and the divine Son of God. And the promise of a future resurrection, anchored in the historical truth of Jesus' own resurrection, fills me with hope, gratitude, and life. I love Scripture. And I love the Jesus of Scripture.

Malcolm Muggeridge discovered the same thing. Toward the end of his life, he observed:

> Contrary to what might be expected, I look back on experiences that at the time seemed especially desolating and painful, with particular satisfaction. Indeed, I can say with complete truthfulness that everything I have learned in my seventy-five years in this world, everything that has truly enhanced and enlightened my existence, has been through affliction and not through happiness, whether pursued or attained .... This, of course, is what the Cross

signifies. And it is the Cross, more than anything else, that has called me inexorably to Christ.[78]

Since Jesus is the divine Son of God who offers us a relationship with God in both this life and the next, we must interpret discipleship as having a holy relationship with God in Christ. In the next chapter, we explore this concept.

Chapter 7

Holy Disciples or Mere Social Activists?

Several years ago, I toured India to witness what missiologists call a "DMM," which is short for "disciple-making movement." I went because I had heard that remarkable, even miraculous, things were happening through the Believer's Church in India.

What I saw astonished me.

Poverty grinds hard among the Indian people—hard enough to surprise me even though I've ministered in many of the world's poorest nations, from Central and South America to Asia, to Africa, to the Middle East. The caste system of India may officially be dead, but in the lives of many ordinary Indians, it is alive and as toxic as ever.

Hundreds of millions of Indians are considered *Dalit* (the "untouchables" of their society). Many see poverty as the fault of the poor—deserved punishment for something they did (maybe even in another life). Crimes against children, women, and others are frequent—widows are still being burned in India, in spite of the fact that something as heinous as burning widows has been illegal since attitudes were changed by Christian missionaries in the 19th century.

The number of people living on the streets, especially in large cities, is astonishing. During a drive through Mother Teresa's beloved Calcutta one night, I saw long stretches where there was no room to walk on the sidewalks because of the vast numbers of people laid out, sleeping and living on the streets. I don't think I could overstate the number of homeless. Leprosy is still an active disease in India, and despite the country's rapidly growing economy and democratic form of government, nearly 200 million Indians officially live below the poverty line—the equivalent of two-thirds of the U.S. population.

All over India, this disciple-making movement was transforming the lives of thousands of these people. I saw the poorest of the poor loved in amazing ways by the local Christians. In some towns, children were fully fed and educated for the very first time. Widows, who are sometimes treated as untouchable, were living together in loving communities, producing goods that supported them and even reaching out in love to others. There were orphanages with literally thousands of children. Other children, who had parents too poor to care for them, were sponsored through the church, with life-saving results. Women often subjected to abuse in India were being uplifted, treated justly, and even encouraged to become leaders. Thousands of wells had been dug across the country, providing fresh water for the first time.

The most humbling thing I did during that tour (if not during my whole life) was to spend a day at a large lepers' colony in the northeast of the country. The church workers there had committed their lives to that colony. Most would never leave. They cared for the lepers—I got to sit in the dirt and feed them myself. They bandaged their wounds, lovingly wrapping, unwrapping, and rewrapping them every day. There were hugs, laughter, and real love—the first time for many of the victims of this treatable disease. I asked the local leader if they were afraid of contracting leprosy themselves.

"No," he explained. "While we might become lepers ourselves, we are not afraid. After all, we follow a Christ who raises people from the dead. Why would we be afraid of leprosy?"

I saw miracles that I'll save for another book. What I want to say here is that all the love, mercy, and justice shown through this movement struck me as something straight out of Acts 2. *This* is the Christian faith I want to have.

But there's a surprising hitch—something so surprising that I had to save it for page two of this chapter or you wouldn't believe it: none of the acts of mercy and justice these Christians showed defined the movement. They believed in justice, but that's not *why* they served. Indeed, they were adamantly opposed to defining their work as "social gospel," and explicitly asked us not to call their work social justice. In fact, they said they don't believe in the social gospel, explaining that the social gospel springs from the same people who gave us atheism, communism, and a variety of philosophies that deny God's sovereignty and opt for godless solutions to human suffering.

Rather, this is a disciple-making movement. Everything these Indian Christians did was only the outgrowth of their real mission. Their real mission was not to help the poor. Rather, to quote first Isaiah and then Jesus, their real mission was to *preach good news* to the poor (Luke 4:18ff, citing Isa. 61:1-2). This Good News is anchored in the fact that Jesus came to save us from our sins and include us in his kingdom. Their mission could be stated in one sentence: to make disciples of all nations. Justice, mercy, love, and social change were the *consequences* of their ministry, not the *goal*.

What these Indian Christians understood, we must also understand. If you make disciples of Jesus, you will get justice, mercy, love, compassion, and even social change. But if you neglect Jesus, focusing on justice, you'll get neither justice nor Jesus.

One of the leaders of Indian Christianity, K.P. Yohannan, explains the consequences of justice without discipleship: "Such [humanist] efforts snatch salvation and true redemption from the poor, condemning them to an eternity in hell."[79] The real problem in India—as is the case in every other nation on earth—is that people are spiritually lost. They are separated from their creator and unwashed by their Savior. Poverty, violence, injustice, and abuse are only symptoms of the problem. And the only cure for the disease is Jesus Christ.

Let me say it again to ensure we all get it: if you make disciples, you'll get justice; if you seek only to make justice, you'll get neither disciples nor justice.

What About Social Justice?

One of the Bible's central concerns is justice. From the Torah and the prophets to the ministry of Jesus and the book of Revelation, God shows his intense concern that people are treated fairly and justly. In Israel, God makes provision for the poor and condemns people who mistreat them. In the prophets, God thunders his disapproval of injustice and abuse, warning, threatening, and eventually punishing those who practice injustice. Jesus goes beyond justice to show mercy to people who actually deserve justice—forgiving an adulteress, eating with a criminal tax collector, and including among his disciples Simon the Zealot. Paul teaches us to care for the poor, and John says that those who do not show mercy to their brothers do not love God. The book of Revelation promises fire and brimstone against Rome for its great injustices and sexual sins (which are a form of injustice). From beginning to end, the Bible is clear: when injustice is allowed to flourish, God will personally set things right, punishing the unjust and bringing salvation to the mistreated.

Indeed, the Christian religion has been one of the greatest sources of justice in human history, not only correcting many of the injustices of paganism but also self-correcting the numerous injustices committed even by the people who call themselves Christian.[80] There can be no mistake here: if the people of God don't practice justice, mercy, peace, and grace, they will not receive it either. We are to be people who care for the poor, the homeless, the imprisoned, the sick, and the marginalized. We are to be a people who stand against the violence perpetrated against those in Syria, Pakistan, and Nigeria. We are to be a people who stand up against the violence of the Latin American drug traders, who now commit more than 10,000 murders per year in Mexico alone. We are to be a people who stand against the massacre that occurs in North America every single minute against those still in the womb. Jesus says that those who do not act with justice and mercy will be thrown away at the resurrection (Matt. 25:31-46).

Yet our acts of justice and mercy are not the core message of Christianity. The core of the gospel is not *our* justice and mercy but *God's* justice and mercy expressed in the truth of the cross. In the atoning death of Jesus, every single human—separated from God through sin—can now be reconciled into a saving relationship with their maker.

Progressive Christianity tends to stand the gospel on its head, doubting the need for the atoning death of Jesus and constructing a civic religion based instead on *our* (rather than God's) claims of justice and mercy. You can hear such sentiments expressed in comments like:

- "All people are basically good."
- "God doesn't require the death of Jesus for our sins; it would be unjust for God to have allowed Jesus to be killed for the sins *we* committed."
- "We don't need to preach the gospel; we just need to show love by bringing justice to the oppressed and provision to the needy."

Let me be clear that I believe our world is in desperate need of justice and mercy, and I'm personally committed to both in my life and in my ministry. Over the years, I have supported a variety of justice and mercy projects with my time and my money—the digging of wells in India, sustainable farming in Tanzania, medical care in Honduras, expanding an orphanage in Brazil, building houses for the poor in Mexico, teaching small business principles to the impoverished in Jamaica, the sponsorship of children in the Dominican Republic and East Africa, the pro-life movement in America, and many others.

In my sermons, I regularly include the theme of racial justice, and our congregation has a spectrum of ethnicities. I serve on the mayor's race relations team and have served on the board of both United Way and one of my community's most charitable organizations. My wife has been the lead manager of one of the largest social justice organizations in our city. My church has as many justice and mercy ministries as any other church in town. Our members support children's homes in Florida, Tennessee, Mexico, and Africa. We have the largest meals-on-wheels ministry in our county and are the official hosts of a full-time summer program for scores of special needs children every year. We have jail ministries, twelve-step programs, back-to-school ministries for under-resourced children, and Christmas giveaways. Whenever there is a disaster, almost anywhere in the world, our church will respond, sometimes by giving tens of thousands of dollars, many times delivering the help personally with open hearts and serving hands. Every day, we give away food to the hungry, and every week, we spend money supporting those in need in our community.

Please don't think I'm bragging here; I say all this to help you understand that I unswervingly embrace the absolute mandate for Christians to practice justice and mercy. I dare not minimize these fundamental values of Scripture. But what I do intend to argue in this chapter is that these mandates cannot *replace* the core of the gospel. Anything that replaces the core of the gospel—which is that Christ died for our sins, was raised to give us life, now reigns as King of kings, and will return to judge all humanity—is heresy and doomed to fail.

Peter Wagner authored more than seventy books, many of them on church growth and evangelism. In some ways, he was the dean of the discipline of evangelism for a whole generation. In his book *Church Growth and the Whole Gospel*, Wagner establishes a truth that has been proven over and over again in history: If we preach the whole gospel of the atoning work of Christ, we will get justice and mercy. But if we focus on social justice without the atoning work of Christ, our efforts will ultimately fail.

For this reason, we must place a premium on evangelism and disciple making.

Many progressives don't realize that we require the gospel to be saved and that acts of justice and mercy flow out of our salvation. Good works are not the source of salvation and they will not bring about the kingdom of God. My church doesn't perform its acts of mercy to establish God's kingdom on earth. Rather, we do these things because God has already established his kingdom in the saving work of Christ.

The difference is subtle but profoundly important and definitive. We do good works not to bring salvation but because salvation has already been brought down in Jesus. We are delighted to practice justice and mercy because God in Christ gives *us* justice and mercy.

Disciple Making Over Activism

Jesus came to make disciples. He performed numerous works of justice and mercy, but these were not his mission. His mission was to make disciples. When one makes disciples, one gets justice and mercy.

And so disciple making is the very first thing Jesus did in his public ministry:

> While walking by the Sea of Galilee, he saw two brothers,
> Simon (who is called Peter) and Andrew his brother,
> casting a net into the sea, for they were fishermen. And he
> said to them, "Follow me, and I will make you fishers of

men." Immediately they left their nets and followed him. And going on from there he saw two other brothers, James the son of Zebedee and John his brother, in the boat with Zebedee their father, mending their nets, and he called them. Immediately they left the boat and their father and followed him. (Matt. 4:18-22)

It was also the last thing Jesus said: "All authority in heaven and on earth has been given to me. Go therefore and make disciples of all nations, baptizing them in the name of the Father and of the Son and of the Holy Spirit, teaching them to observe all that I have commanded you. And behold, I am with you always, to the end of the age" (Matt. 28:18 20).

Almost every time the final words of Jesus are recorded in the New Testament, some sort of disciple-making message is given:

- Jesus ends the Gospel of Matthew by telling us to go make disciples of all nations (Matthew 28:19).
- The longer ending of Mark says, "Go into all the world and proclaim the gospel to the whole creation. Whoever believes and is baptized will be saved, but whoever does not believe will be condemned" (Mark 16:15-16).
- Luke ends his Gospel by quoting Jesus: "Thus it is written, that the Christ should suffer and on the third day rise from the dead, and that repentance and forgiveness of sins should be proclaimed in his name to all nations, beginning from Jerusalem. You are witnesses of these things" (Luke 24:46-48).
- In Acts, Jesus' final words are these: "But you will receive power when the Holy Spirit has come upon you, and you will be my witnesses in Jerusalem and in all Judea and Samaria, and to the end of the earth" (Acts 1:8).
- And John's Gospel begins to end with this commission: "'Peace be with you. As the Father has sent me, even so I am sending you.' And when he had said this, he breathed on them and said to them, 'Receive the Holy Spirit'" (John 20:21-22).

For those who are measuring, all these words are in red letters. As Jesus says about his own mission: "[T]he Son of Man came to seek and to save the lost" (Luke 19:10). Everything between the opening of Matthew and its close is about making disciples—faith-filled followers of Jesus. Though the term "Christian" is a solid, proud term, it only appears three times in the Bible. Versions of the word "disciple" appear nearly three hundred times. And it's worth noting that though the Bible is deeply concerned about justice, the term "social justice" never appears in the Bible. It was only recently coined.[81]

Jesus made disciples by entering into the lives of a handful of individuals for the purpose of making them like him—precisely what disciple making actually is.

Mentoring or apprenticing a handful of followers was the standard way of educating, and therefore making social change, in the ancient world. Socrates mentored Plato. Plato mentored Aristotle. Rabbis mentored their *talmidim* (the Hebrew word for disciples). Moses mentored Joshua (Deut. 34:9). Elijah mentored Elisha (2 Kgs. 2:12-15). Peter mentored Mark (1 Pet. 5:13). Paul mentored Timothy (1 Tim. 3:10-11). Older women are taught to mentor younger women (Tit. 2:3-5). And everyone is taught to mentor others, so that they can, in turn, mentor others (2 Tim. 2:2).

After the close of the New Testament, disciples continued the work of Jesus. The apostle John discipled Ignatius, Papias, and Polycarp. Polycarp discipled Tertullian and Irenaeus. Tertullian discipled Cyprian, and Irenaeus discipled Hippolytus. And so forth.

The four Gospels share vivid pictures of Jesus cultivating a deep and intense relationship with twelve men. A comment by Mark states an often-missed disciple-making principle: Jesus, we're told, appointed the twelve "*that they might be with him* and that he might send them out to preach and to have authority to cast out demons" (Mark 3:14-15, italics mine). Jesus ate dinner with them and lived with them (Matt. 9:10). He pulled them from the crowds to give them private training (Mark 4:33-34). He taught them to do ministry and to preach (Matt. 10:5ff; 6:37). He took three of them into a world of private miracles (Matt. 17:1) and was so close to one that John is described as leaning on Jesus' chest during supper (John 13:23-25).[82]

Jesus came to seek and save the lost (Luke 19:10), but he did this by making disciples. Disciple making is the main thing, not good works or social justice. Investing in the lives of others for the purpose of bringing out the Jesus in them is the only real way to make lasting change in the world. At the end of the day, hearts must be changed, and they are only changed when they are handcrafted. We believe that Jesus' message was perfect. In the same way, we should believe that his method was perfect.

Several years ago, Mike Breen, who helped found the missional community model of church planting—a model that uses social justice as a primary tool—wrote an article entitled "Why the Missional Movement Will Fail."[83] It was a bit jolting to have one of the founders of the missional movement declare that it will not succeed. But Breen is clear that unless disciple making is the main thing, social justice and missional emphases simply cannot succeed. In the article Breen wrote:

> Sending people out to do mission is to send them out
> to a war zone. Discipleship is not only the boot camp to
> train them for the front lines, but the hospital when they
> get wounded and the off-duty time they need to rest and
> recuperate. When we don't disciple people the way Jesus
> and the New Testament talked about, we are sending
> them out without armor, weapons or training. This is mass
> carnage waiting to happen.[84]

Social mission without full-throttled disciple making is, Breen explains, like a car without an engine. Jesus changed the world by making disciples, who made disciples, who made more disciples.

Repentance From Personal Sin

Because Jesus' mission on earth was to make individual disciples, he called and still calls people to individual repentance. I've already pointed out instances of this in the Gospels. Disciple making is personal, individual, and one-on-one. Disciples are always handcrafted, never mass-produced. And so it's worth noting that Jesus hardly conducted his earthly ministry as a 21st-century social activist. He confronted the religious hypocrisy of the Sadducees and Pharisees, but he didn't confront them as politicians so much as misinformed theologians.

More telling, Jesus never argues against any public policy, stating rather that his kingdom is not of this world (John 18:36). Imperial Rome was filled with social injustices, and Jesus knew that quite well. He taught people not to go along with these systems, but he never protested the systems themselves. No marches. No demonstrations. No burning of Roman standards. No battles over court appointees. Tiberius Caesar was a horrible person—one of the most perverted, violent, and cruel men in history. But Jesus never confronted his policies. Jesus never even confronted Rome with all its evils. When asked about paying taxes to Caesar, he simply showed them a picture of Tiberius on a coin and said, "Give him what is his" (Mark 12:17).

Instead of challenging Rome's social institutions, Jesus confronted individuals and the religious establishment with their sins, called them to repentance, and demanded that they embrace him as Lord. Jesus knew—and this is very important—that if he changed enough lives individually and from the heart, Rome's evils would collapse on themselves. And this is exactly what happened. When Christianity grew large enough, many of the empire's evils were banished by the emperors themselves—everything from adultery and the gladiatorial games to infanticide and abortion. The Roman world was not changed by protests and marches; it was changed by the making of millions of disciples.

This is very different from the social project of progressives. While they might use the phrase "disciple," what progressives often mean is someone who agrees with their social causes. They tend to believe that Jesus focused on social institutions and was much less concerned with individuals. This explains why progressive churches typically speak very little about the very real and destructive sins of their members, and instead speak with a fire in their belly about union laws in Illinois, the ice caps in the polar seas, and the appointment of judges on the West Coast. So a man can abandon the wife he swore to be faithful to in order to live sexually with another man, and in progressive Episcopalianism he becomes a hero and a bishop. His personal sins are irrelevant so long as he takes the right social positions.[85]

Again, I'm not suggesting that there is no place for social and political action for Christians; there most certainly is. I've sometimes advocated political positions that I thought demanded Christian attention. But I also advocate that Christians generally practice modesty about our political and social positions. As Carl Henry warned some years back, churches do not have the mandate or jurisdiction, and most churches aren't sufficiently competent to know what good policy actually is.[86] I can say with conviction that most pastors and theologians I know have no idea what good statecraft entails. Progressives will pick some recent policy proposal out of a *thousand* possible policy options—generally a policy proposal advocated by Hollywood or by university elites—then announce through their Facebook or Twitter accounts that anyone who doesn't support that *one particular option* among the thousand policy options available is evil, racist, sexist, homophobic, and deplorable. Liberal congressional members call for a 3.7 percent increase in Head Start funding. Fiscally conservative members call for a 2.9 percent increase. Progressive Christians hit the streets with protests and rage-filled tirades about how evil the conservatives are—evidently believing that Jesus demands a 3.7 percent increase over, say, 3.68 percent or 3.77 percent. The narrowness, short-sightedness, and superficiality of defining the Christian faith in such a way is breathtaking, and trite.

I should also add that many crowds are easily manipulated toward emotional causes and reckless demography, which can make social activism imbalanced and even dangerous. As Malcolm Muggeridge says:

> Jesus himself, even in his obscurity, dreaded the gathering of crowds, and where possible avoided them. Everything in Christianity that matters is from individual to individual; collectivities belong to the Devil, and so easily respond to his persuasion. The Devil is a demagogue and sloganeer; Jesus was, and is, concerned with individual souls, with the Living Word. What he gives us is truth carried on the wings of love, not slogans carried on the thrust of power.[87]

And we should add that forms of social action in the name of justice have had a very mixed track record. History, especially in the 20th century, is filled with examples of people aiming for justice without Christ and ending with atrocious forms of injustice:

- The Soviet Union sloganeered on the phrase "workers of the world unite." But seventy years of godless socialism cost the lives of millions of ordinary, innocent people, while oligarchs and politicians dined on caviar and capitalist cognac.
- Mao Zedong, former chairman of the Communist Party in China, launched a social justice revolution in China, perhaps for good reasons. But soon, the godless ideals of his utopia devolved into the largest mass murder in history—as many as fifty million people were deliberately starved to death in the name of justice during the "Great Leap Forward."
- The Khmer Rouge in Cambodia seized power for the purpose of granting equality to all Cambodians. It ended with a fifth of the population murdered.
- In the French Revolution of the 18th century, God was banished in favor of *liberté, égalité, et fraternité*. Without the cross, the guillotine became the symbol of social justice.
- In the U.S., the call for women's justice was originally Christian, but when it veered from its Christian roots, it ended up with the murder of millions of babies in the abhorrent practice of abortion—now a holy sacrament among progressives.[88]

Because they naively believe that such horrors are mere examples of social justice *misapplied*, liberal progressives generally downplay these crimes against humanity—as they're currently doing with places like Venezuela, Cuba, Nicaragua, North Korea, the Middle East, and other areas known for human rights violations.[89] But what if these are actually evidences of the inevitable consequence of any social justice movement that fails to put God first and doesn't call for repentance for personal sin? What if Pascal (an orthodox Christian) was right? "Man is neither angel nor beast, and unhappily whoever wants to act the angel, acts the beast."

Jesus came to make disciples, and disciples will practice justice and mercy, both on a personal and a social level. But practicing justice is not the focus of discipleship; it is the product of it. In the same way, holiness is a sign of true discipleship. But holiness has fallen on hard times among progressives. So in the next chapter we must discuss holiness and following Jesus.

Chapter 8
Loving God with a Holy Life

One of the delights—and burdens—of local ministry is the opportunity to become deeply involved in the lives of real people. Two pastoral stories, both of them true, will demonstrate what I want to say in this chapter.

Some years back, a young teenager asked her mother if she could be baptized by me. The excited mother called and made an appointment so we could discuss it. Her mother is a loveable person, but when she was young her father abandoned her. There has been a deep hole in her life ever since, which she has tried to fill in a variety of unhealthy ways, including with multiple relationships with men. The father of the teenage girl I was to baptize was one of those men. He had long since left, and now the teen lived with an enormous hole in *her* heart too.

Ignoring all this so I could honor the girl, I simply asked the girl to tell me why she wanted to be baptized. Suddenly, her smile went away, and she exploded in sobbing tears, shaking uncontrollably. After a few seconds, she lifted her face and looked at me crying and stuttering, "I just want somebody to love me." My heart broke for her, and all I could think of was how we North Americans had managed to build a world where it is okay to abandon one's child and leave a permanent hole in her heart.

We must be honest here. The young girl who bitterly wept for love is not an accidental victim. She is, instead, the victim of an unjust and unholy relational system that North Americans have built which says that it's okay for two people to enter into a casual sexual relationship, and then it's okay for one or both of them to abandon their children—all in pursuit of happiness (or shall we say, "authenticity"). The sexual mores of America constitute perhaps the greatest injustice of our time. Though the father of the girl may not have been a progressive—he probably had no religion at all—his cruel and unjust abandonment of his own daughter was abetted by the sexual revolution, which suggests that sex is a private matter whose consequences must be borne by somebody else. The sexual revolution is one of the greatest social projects of American progressivism, and so the damage the sexual revolution has wrought upon Americans must be laid at the feet of progressivism.

A second story: An older member of my church came to me several years ago with a gleam in his eye. I had known him for years but not very well.

"Thank you, thank you, thank you so very much," he exclaimed as he ran into me in the church building. I had no idea what he was talking about.

He explained, "I have struggled with alcohol for years. I have been in and out of treatment. I have tried everything. My addiction has cost my family dearly, and they are still paying for it. But over the last year, I have been in the church's Celebrate Recovery ministry, and I have now been sober for more than a year—for the first time in my adult life. And I did it because in Celebrate Recovery's use of the Bible, I found Jesus. I found grace. I found strength to recover. Please tell everyone my story!"

This man's recovery and subsequent holy life was the result of a personal relationship with the Savior. No public policy had helped him. No activism. Not even a good set of ethics, rituals, or activist principles. What saved him was a personal, holy relationship with Jesus Christ. Both of these stories emphasize the need individuals have for the salvation Jesus offers and the value of holiness. A lack of holiness brings intense pain—as in the case of the young woman. And the practice of holiness brings great joy—as in the case of the older man.

Holiness is not a scourge on the Christian faith. It is a core element of our faith, and it is a source of great joy. "Blessed is the one you choose .... *We shall be satisfied* with the goodness of your house, the holiness of your temple!" (Ps. 65:4).

Holiness and Personal Sin

Jesus calls disciples to personal repentance so that we can be justified and purified by God. God grants us holiness so we can have a right relationship with him, but he expects us to live consistent with that holiness. For this reason disciples of Jesus must commit to personal holiness.

In recent decades, holiness has fallen on hard times among progressives, but it is actually a central theme for the Christian faith. Nearly 700 times the Bible uses the term. At its heart, to be holy is to conduct yourself in a sacred way—in the same ways God conducts himself. Holiness often describes how we should approach relationships our relationship with God (as in prayer, fasting, praise, and the like), our relationships with others (as in sexual purity, respectful treatment, and love), and our relationship to ourselves (as in discipline, joy, and honesty).

The beauty of the work of Christ is that he calls profane people, then invites them to become holy. The apostle Peter, who sat at the feet of Jesus, saw holiness as a central theme for Christ followers:

- "As obedient children, do not be conformed to the passions of your former ignorance, but as he who called you is holy, you also be holy in all your conduct, since it's written, 'You shall be holy, for I am holy'" (1 Peter 1:14-16).
- "But you are a chosen race, a royal priesthood, a holy nation, a people for his own possession, that you may proclaim the excellencies of him who called you out of darkness into his marvelous light. Once you were not a people, but now you are God's people; once you had not received mercy, but now you have received mercy" (1 Peter 2:9-10).

And Jesus himself emphasizes that his work is about personal holiness:

I am Jesus whom you are persecuting. But rise and stand upon your feet, for I have appeared to you for this purpose, to appoint ... to open their eyes, so that they may turn from darkness to light and from the power of Satan to God, that they may receive forgiveness of sins and a place among those who are *sanctified* [that is, *made holy*] by faith in me. (Acts 26:15-18, red letters)

Holiness should characterize the collective Christian community, but it actually begins with the individual. It begins when we personally commit to being like God in all we do. When individuals are holy, institutions become holy.

In the Old Testament, holiness can describe numerous things—sacrifices, furniture, ethics, land, actions, people, hairstyles, and the like. But by the time we get to the New Testament, we learn that holiness is actually grounded in one simple principle: love. Since living a holy life means living devoted to God, and since God is himself love, holiness is grounded in love. So Jesus commands us to love one another (John 13:34-35). When we love one another, we act toward each other as God does—caring, forgiving, serving, and even rescuing each other. This is holiness: to treat others with the same kind of love that God offers them.

But love for others is actually the *second* fundamental of holiness. Even more important than loving others, Jesus teaches us, is loving God. Ultimate holiness occurs when we commit to loving God with all we are (Mark 12:30). And what does this mean? The answer is both simple and difficult. It is simple in that it means submitting to God in everything we do. This isn't hard to understand. But it is difficult in its application. As I said above, we have broken wills, and we are, by nature, self-serving creatures. Unredeemed, most of us want God's will so long as it agrees with our will. We want a God who forgives us when we sin. We want a God who loves us even though we're imperfect. We want a God who gives us stuff, who brings us lovers, who showers us with blessings, who makes us happy. We want a God who fixes what we think is wrong with the world.

But the real challenge of loving God occurs when we find that God's will is not often our will. At that point, we're profoundly challenged to ask whether or not we love God. What about when God tells us to stop loving money? What about when God tells us to love our enemies? What about when God condemns our selfishness? And what about when God teaches sexual purity? It's here that we discover whether we really love God.

This makes Mark 7:21-23 an important text, for it gives the longest "red letter" list of sins that render us unclean before God: "For from within, out of the heart of man, come evil thoughts, sexual immorality, theft, murder, adultery, coveting, wickedness, deceit, sensuality, envy, slander, pride, foolishness. All these evil things come from within, and they defile a person."

It's worth noting that Jesus addresses these as personal, individual sins, and even though groups of people (governments, social structures, and the like) can be guilty of them as well, Jesus is most concerned about what's in the hearts of individuals. It's what he actually says. That's because, again, Jesus changes social structures by changing people's hearts through the call of discipleship.

We should pause on this Markan text for another moment to see the central concern of Jesus: his interest is in keeping disciples "clean," or "holy." Sin is many things in the Bible—missing the mark, acting wrongly, committing a crime. But it is also uncleanness, impurity, and unholiness. And in three different ways, Jesus addresses sexual sin as a matter of unholiness (immorality, adultery, lewdness). Sexual sin is unholy because sexual sin is unloving. At its heart, sexual sin is the sin of using other people, and contrary to the claims of many progressives, sexual sin is not a victimless crime. In fact, sexual sin may well be the greatest injustice of our time.

Sexual Holiness and Progressivism

Nothing in the 21st century seems to rile progressives in the same way as does the apostolic teaching about sex and gender. Biblical Christians are often accused of obsessing over sex while ignoring matters of justice, greed, or poverty. I think the accusation is sometimes valid. But we must acknowledge that it wasn't biblical Christians who made sex a defining issue in the decadent West—it was progressives. Theirs was the sexual revolution—a movement that reduces the lofty concept of freedom to little more than having sex with anyone you please. To quote again from Muggeridge on liberalism, "The orgasm has replaced the Cross as the focus of longing and the image of fulfillment."[90]

Perhaps the greatest social injustice of our time is the injustice done against the family by the sexual ethic of progressive theology. Virtually every social indicator of well-being in America has been in rapid decline since the sexual revolution of the 1960s, as family after family is undermined by the removal of sexual guardrails meticulously built since the days of the late Empire. Elites continue to navigate these age-old boundaries with some aptitude, but the masses of Americans have paid an enormous cost for the sexual ethics advocated by leftist elites.[91]

Destroyed marriages, broken hearts, millions of fatherless children, sexually confused teens, millions of abortions—these disfigure the beautiful gift God gives us in the divine formula of one man and one woman, in a faithful married covenant for life. And I'm not including here the rise of crime, the explosion of drug use, the mass number of suicides, the mental illnesses, the social disorder, and the gutted communities that have resulted from the sexual escapades of theological progressivism.[92] Just the enormous emotional and social toll of fatherless children alone is enough to break your heart.

In his helpful book focusing on the 20th century, *Five Lies of the Century*, author David Moore writes: "From relationships, education, to mental instability, to crime, one factor looms as the most significant contributor: a home without a dad."[93] And we must be clear here: the damage done to millions of children by the collapse of the American family is the direct result of *deliberate* progressive values and policies.

I'm aware that the progressives seek to find a new way to read sex and gender in the Bible, but when you read the many efforts to escape simple, biblical teachings on sexual purity, you can see that what's really going on is a hermeneutic of convenience. Progressives want sex and gender to be fluid, so they search for ways to reinterpret the Bible, to call sections of it "merely cultural," or simply to dismiss those sections that disagree with their beliefs or feelings. They really don't need an interpretation; they've already made up their minds that sexual self-expression is a higher value than holiness and faithfulness to God.

Rosaria Butterfield was a liberal, Marxist, feminist, lesbian professor at an elite university in the Northeast. She was filled with rage toward the Bible and the Christians who take it seriously. Some years back, she decided to write an essay against the evils she thought she saw in biblical Christianity. Still holding to her biases, she began to visit a local church.

It took a while, but through the patience of a godly couple, she began to see that the Bible is actually a liberating book and that she had been looking at Christianity through the lenses of 20th-century liberalism.

Early on, she visited a left-leaning pastor who told her she didn't need to worry about her lifestyle—sections of the Bible that contradict her can be dismissed. Even as a non-believer, she later stated, she knew that the pastor was being dishonest with the Bible.

Eventually, God got hold of Dr. Butterfield, and she walked away from her former life, joining a church serious about the Bible and committing her life to Jesus Christ. Her books are some of the best I've ever read. The thrill she feels when she obeys the Word of God is contagious. She is the smartest person in any room she enters, and she sees the beauty, the power, and the truthfulness of God's way. She has risked her career—and occasionally her life—by writing and speaking on the call of God for sexual and gender holiness. Oddly, her greatest critics are not unbelievers. They are progressive Christians who hate her message of loving God enough to submit to his Word, even when it's hard. They often argue that God isn't concerned with your sex or gender, so long as you're faithful. But faithfulness is the last thing on the minds of progressives—when is the last time you heard a progressive criticize anyone for being unfaithful? What progressives actually value is permissiveness, not faithfulness.

When Paul explains how a culture can fall deeply into moral blindness, he tells us that sexual sin is typically the beginning point:

> Therefore God gave them up in the lusts of their hearts
> to impurity, to the dishonoring of their bodies among
> themselves, because they exchanged the truth about God
> for a lie and worshiped and served the creature rather
> than the Creator, who is blessed forever! Amen. For this
> reason God gave them up to dishonorable passions. For
> their women exchanged natural relations for those that are
> contrary to nature; and the men likewise gave up natural
> relations with women and were consumed with passion
> for one another, men committing shameless acts with men
> and receiving in themselves the due penalty for their error.
> And since they did not see fit to acknowledge God, God
> gave them up to a debased mind to do what ought not to
> be done. (Rom. 1:24-28)

These are hard words, but they are true—whether we want them to be or not. On the cusp of the fall of the socialist Berlin Wall and the end of the Cold War, which he helped bring about, Pope John Paul II wrote the classic *Veritatis Splendor* ("The Splendor of the Truth"). His arguments are simple and powerful. Truth exists, whether we like it or not. We don't create truth; we find it. And we cannot change it when we don't like it. But if we submit to it, we will find God. Truth is the only path to happiness. Or, as Jesus himself put it, "The truth will set you free" (John 8:32). But the reverse is also true. The lies of sexual sin produce bondage.

Orthodox, biblical, historical Christian teaching about sexual purity and gender is fundamental to social justice because sex is a load-bearing wall in human wellbeing. Sex was given to us as a gift from God—a form of superglue for husbands and wives that repeatedly unites them in a re-enactment of the oneness God gives us in marriage. But superglue must be handled with care—spread it around casually or put it on the wrong things and people get torn up badly. When we continually desecrate the sacred act of sex, civilization begins to crumble. Jesus gives the timeless truth: "Have you not read that he who created them from the beginning made them male and female, and said, 'Therefore a man shall leave his father and his mother and hold fast to his wife, and they shall become one flesh?' So they are no longer two but one flesh. What therefore God has joined together, let not man separate" (Matt. 19:4-6). And the truth will set you free.

Note the connection in the Scriptures between holiness and sexual purity:

- "Flee from sexual immorality. Every other sin a person commits is outside the body, but the sexually immoral person sins against his own body. Or do you not know that your body is a temple of the Holy Spirit within you, whom you have from God? You are not your own, for you were bought with a price. So glorify God in your body" (1 Corinthians 6:18-20).
- "For this is the will of God, your sanctification: that you abstain from sexual immorality; that each one of you know how to control his own body in holiness and honor, not in the passion of lust like the Gentiles who do not know God; that no one transgress and wrong his brother in this matter, because the Lord is an avenger in

all these things, as we told you beforehand and solemnly warned you. For God has not called us for impurity, but in holiness" (1 Thessalonians 4:3-7).

- "Therefore, if anyone cleanses himself from what is dishonorable, he will be a vessel for honorable use, set apart as holy, useful to the master of the house, ready for every good work. So flee youthful passions and pursue righteousness, faith, love, and peace ..." (2 Timothy 2:21-22).

- "The time that is past suffices for doing what the Gentiles want to do, living in sensuality, passions, drunkenness, orgies, drinking parties, and lawless idolatry. With respect to this they are surprised when you do not join them in the same flood of debauchery, and they malign you; but they will give account to him who is ready to judge the living and the dead" (1 Peter 4:3-5).

- "But I have this against you, that you tolerate that woman Jezebel, who calls herself a prophetess and is teaching and seducing my servants to practice sexual immorality and to eat food sacrificed to idols. I gave her time to repent, but she refuses to repent of her sexual immorality. Behold, I will throw her onto a sickbed, and those who commit adultery with her I will throw into great tribulation, unless they repent of her works, and I will strike her children dead. And all the churches will know that I am he who searches mind and heart, and I will give to each of you as your works deserve" (Revelation 2:20-23).

- "Behold, I am coming soon, bringing my recompense with me, to repay everyone for what he has done. I am the Alpha and the Omega, the first and the last, the beginning and the end. Blessed are those who wash their robes, so that they may have the right to the tree of life and that they may enter the city by the gates. Outside are the dogs and sorcerers and the sexually immoral and murderers and idolaters, and everyone who loves and practices falsehood" (Revelation 22:12-15).

God has called us to share in his holiness (Heb. 12:10). His call is for us to become a holy people (1 Cor. 3:17). And our love for others—our ethics, our mercy, and our grace, must all spring from holiness. As Paul

says, "Put to death therefore what is earthly in you: sexual immorality ….
Put on then, as God's chosen ones, *holy and beloved,* compassionate hearts,
kindness, humility, meekness, and patience …" (Col. 3:5, 12).

Sexual sin is not the biggest sin one can commit, but it is a particularly
unholy sin, because it is unloving toward others and, ultimately, unloving
toward God. So let me say this clearly: whenever popular bloggers and
Christian authors experience a "conversion" from apostolic Christianity
and toss out what the sacred Scriptures say about sex in order to accommodate progressive sexual mores, they are not only committing a grave sin.
They are leading others away from the holiness to which God calls them.
And God is watching.

For this reason, we must clearly reject the teachings of authors, bloggers, and speakers who constantly write about "inclusiveness" and "wel-
coming environments" without also writing about repentance from sinful
behavior—even warm, witty, and winsome authors. Jesus calls all people
to come *and repent.* Progressives call people to come and *continue to sin.*
Christ is inclusive—of everyone who comes to him and repents. He repeatedly makes it clear that he will *not* include those who refuse to repent of
their sins (as in Matt. 7:21-27). And those who teach others to abandon biblical sexual ethics are following the paths of Jezebel (Rev. 2:20, red letters).

Love Rightly Understood

Thus, loving God first means subordinating our values, our preferences, and our beliefs to those taught to us in God's Word. But this shouldn't
be a punishing thing. As the apostle reminds us, "For this is the love of
God, that we keep his commandments. And his commandments are not
burdensome" (1 John 5:3). When we love God enough to set aside our will
and adopt his, inexpressible peace and joy fill our hearts. I believe that's
why so many biblical disciples, scholars, mystics, and martyrs have died
with expressions of joy on their faces.

Loving God is the first commandment, and the second is to love others as ourselves. When Jesus calls disciples, he immediately invites them
into the circle of other disciples—not to rowdy crowds of protestors but
to a holy and compassionate fellowship of Christ followers, which the rest
of the Bible calls the church. This community of believers forms the pillar

and ground of the truth of Jesus: a treasury of the inheritance God wants to give the entire world (cf., 1 Tim. 3:16-17; Rom. 8:16-17; 1 Pet. 1:3-5).

This community forms around the teachings of the apostles, around prayer, around communal meals and fellowship, around shared praise of God and shared sacrifice, and around witnessing Christ to the world (Acts 2:42ff). It's a communion built on love for God and love for others. Its members are devoted to one another and recognize that they are the family of God. As Jesus replied when his physical family had come to get him, "'Who is my mother, and who are my brothers?' And stretching out his hand toward his disciples, he said, 'Here are my mother and my brothers! For whoever does the will of my Father in heaven is my brother and sister and mother'" (Matt. 12:48-50).

As early as Matthew 16, Jesus uses the term "church" to describe this community. It's a term that simply means "gathering" or "assembly." But in the hands of God, the church becomes a sacred assembly—one given the task of building up its members so as to reach maturity in Christ (Eph. 4:10-16). Because it's holy, the church is called the body of Christ, the temple of the Holy Spirit, and the bride of Christ.

Of course, the primary motivation within the church is love. But it is love rightly understood. In post-modernism, the term "love" often devolves into mere *acceptance* or *tolerance*—or even *indulgence*. Non-judgmentalism may be relational capital the elite can afford, but it leaves the vast majority of humans with no clear direction for living dignified, Christlike lives—hence, the increasing dysfunctionality of post-Christian America. Removing the social and cultural guardrails in the name of "inclusiveness" is a luxury for the elite. For the masses, life careens off the road when there are no rails.

Biblical, Christian love is much richer—and much harder—than non-judgmentalism. Biblical love is a commitment to the well-being of others as defined by God. To love people as Christ loves them is to do the hard work of being honest with them about their sin and then helping them escape sin's power. As Peter Hubbard points out, love is not portrayed in the Bible as "the ring of power that makes us invisible to moral confrontation."[94] The concept that "if you love me, you will affirm my lifestyle no matter what" is a product of the TV program *Glee*, not of God. If we love others, we will be honest enough with them to show them a better way than the way of fallenness.

There is nothing loving about telling sinners they are okay in their sin, just as there is nothing loving about giving cocaine to a drug addict. Indulgence and misplaced tolerance are not biblical love, and they will not solve humanity's problems. Real love—Christ's kind of love—"does not rejoice at wrongdoing, but rejoices with the truth" (1 Cor. 13:6). God's love does not ignore our sin, but seeks to atone for it, as Romans reminds us: "God shows his love for us in that while we were still sinners, Christ died for us" (Rom. 5:8). Real love pursues sinners to rescue them from their sin: "My brothers, if anyone among you wanders from the truth and someone brings him back, let him know that whoever brings back a sinner from his wandering will save his soul from death and will cover a multitude of sins" (Jam. 5:19-20).

So to love others as we love ourselves is to be willing to speak honestly about sin and salvation and to be willing to pay the price for others—the price of hard work, emotional fatigue, and even public rejection. Christians aren't known by their tweets; they are known by their love.

What is Our Mission?

Doing good is not the ultimate mission of following Jesus. This is an important point because it would be easy to think that our mission is to bring about the kingdom of God here on earth. This is most certainly *not* our mission. We have no ability to bring about God's kingdom; that's his job. Rather, our job is to act like people who are *already* in his kingdom.

And we must be modest here. Scripture and human experience have proven over and over again that this world is broken, and there is only so much optimism we can afford. We can do good; we can make the world a better place; we can help alleviate the suffering of many. With God's help, we've already done a lot of this.

But we must recognize that this world is not going to last, and there are limits to how much goodness can flourish in a world where human will is broken. God's ultimate plan is not to bring about a utopia here through government, public policy, or social activism. We must say this clearly because liberal progressivism has always been something of a state religion—a version of Christianity designed to make good citizens and good government. This is why progressives always gravitate toward politics, government, and social action for solutions. Look at the websites of the mainline Protestant denominations in America, and you'll see hundreds of statements about public policy, government, and social issues. Liberals once lectured conservatives about mixing church and state, but no religion in America is as willing to ally itself with politics as is progressive Christianity.

For an example of this, one only needs to peruse the Twitter accounts of such progressives as Shane Claiborne, Rachel Held Evans, and Brian McLaren. Almost daily, these leaders tweet messages that seem full of rage against a host of non-progressive causes and people. Virtually every theological view they tweet is a collectivist view—a left-leaning statement about public policy and politics. These progressives rarely address the individual sins Jesus and the apostles addressed. But they storm on and on about congress, immigration policy, and whatever other cause the secular left has discovered.

God's ultimate plan is not to use politics, government, and social justice to create a millennial reign on this earth. Rather, his plan is to destroy this earth and bring about a new creation—a new heaven and a new earth where he dwells among us. Our job is to begin living here already as citizens of this new world. We do good not to create the kingdom but because God has already made us citizens of his kingdom.[95] The kingdom of God belongs to God, not to us. And all our *shalom*, justice, and goodness put together will never bring about God's kingdom.

What, then, is our mission? Well, our purpose as humans is to worship God. But our mission is to give the world Jesus—it is to make disciples of all nations, where the emphasis is not on the "making" part of the equation but rather the "disciple" part. In other words, since being a disciple of Jesus is the goal of this life, leading others to discipleship must be our mission. And so we take up the task of proclaiming to every single person that they have a Savior and Lord who wants to restore a broken relationship with them, and who will lead them to a life of grace and holiness here, and a rich eternal life hereafter. This is who we are. Anything less than this misses the mark. Anything less than this is not the gospel. Anything less than this is some other god's story.

If we deny this mission, God will move on to other people, and we will fail. And all over North America, progressive denominations are, in fact, failing. To this final observation we now turn.

Chapter 9

The Future of Progressive Christianity

The orthodox Jew and social philosopher Will Herberg converted the liberal theology professor Thomas Oden to orthodox Christianity, starting with the words, "You will remain theologically uneducated until you study Athanasius, Augustine, and Aquinas." Reminding Oden that one day he would be judged for the shoddy theology he had taught, Herberg went further: "If you are ever going to become a credible theologian instead of a know-it-all pundit, you had best restart your life on firmer ground. You are not a theologian except in name only, even if you are paid to be one."[96]

The brilliant professor Herberg made the bold accusation against Oden during a casual conversation at Drew University. He accused the professor of throwing his life away through an ignorance of real Christianity. Scales fell from Oden's eyes. He felt shame, embarrassment, and conviction.

Up until this point, Oden had been a leading North American theologian. He had studied under Richard Niebuhr, receiving his Ph.D. in religion from Yale University. Oden had already gained numerous accolades for his work on religion, psychology, and social causes. Before his death, he would go on to teach religion at Yale University, SMU, Drew University, Heidelberg University, Princeton Theological Seminary, Lomonosov University, and the Pontifical Gregorian University in Rome.

Oden had already interacted with numerous luminaries in religion—at one point being chastised by Karl Barth for measuring the Christian faith by the decadent Western standards of personal authenticity. He would meet presidents, theologians, and the world's leading philosophers. He even once shared a private communion with the Pope.

Born in 1931, Oden grew up Methodist, but the brand of Methodism he embraced was stridently progressive. Even as a teenager sent to youth camp, he was taught that personal salvation—such as that taught by Acts and Paul—was hopelessly passé, and that social reform was the true call of Christianity. Soon, the leaders in his circles were cheering him on for his Marxist, liberationist, and non-orthodox views. His heroes became Saul Alinsky, Ho Chi Minh, Friedrich Nietzsche, and Freud.

Oden remained in church but was unable to read the Bible or repeat the Apostles' Creed without embarrassment and enormous mental gymnastics. He had to deny—if not in his speech, at least in his heart—the very words that had once given his denomination life, power, and beauty. By the time he was in his early forties, Oden had embraced every liberal cause that came to define progressivism, believing that anything old was inherently wrong and instead embracing every new social movement that came along.

Until Herberg called him out. Herberg had grown up a leftist, but abandoned the illusions of the left when he saw the damage it had done, especially in Eastern Europe and Asia, where it had actually been put into practice. Herberg returned to the Judaism of his ancestors and spent much of the rest of his life debunking leftist ideologies. When he saw Oden's obsession with progressive imagination and utopianism, he challenged him.

Soon, Oden began to feel shame over his constant lust for the new, his ignorance of historic orthodox Christianity, and his love for progressivism. He began to rediscover the power of the apostolic witness and to take the words of Scripture seriously. He found that Scripture makes sense of life and brings power to faith. He fell in love with the great Christian thinkers—even founding a movement he called "paleo-orthodoxy" (the choice to live faithfully to the Christian treasure handed to us by the great founders and interpreters of our faith).

His conversion was so thorough that Oden became one of the 20th and 21st century's most articulate and powerful defenders of the sacred truths of the apostolic witness.[97] He once dreamed, he liked to say, that his tombstone would read: "Here lies Thomas Oden, who contributed nothing new to theology."

Soon, he had repented of his theological progressivism. He saw that the sexual revolution had destroyed the lives of millions, that abortion was the killing of the innocent for the convenience of others, that Marxism only makes sense on university campuses, that Nietzsche's teaching had totalitarian consequences, that DNA screams of intelligent design, that liberals routinely gave moral passes to the social evils of collectivist regimes, and that Freudian psychoanalysis was actually less effective than mere spontaneous recovery.

He even went so far as to retract many of his former progressive beliefs in public, leading to rage and hatred against him by those who typically argued for inclusiveness and tolerance. He spent much of the last 40 years of his life doing reparations for the damage he believed his previous work had done. He found partners in orthodox Christianity all over the world. Indeed, before his death, Oden came to discover that there was an entire world of Bible-believing, orthodox Christians outside of North America. These Christians were repulsed by the elite, white liberalism of North American Christianity. Oden was especially drawn to Africa where he found ancient Christian communities, who—by the millions—were in love with the Bible and orthodox Christianity. They had remained faithful for millennia. One of his last books advocated African forms of Christianity.[98]

Oden was a generous, loving, humble, and kind-hearted man. But he saw through the dangers of theological progressivism, writing: "We face an adversary who presents himself as a friend, and we cannot afford to be naïve about this combat."[99] Or, to put it another way, Oden found that in the Christian religion we get a choice: life or death.

The Death of Mainline Progressivism

Everywhere you turn, theologically progressive churches are dying. This is true even though the flight of evangelicals to progressivism is artificially slowing the speed of the decline. The liberal wings of Presbyterianism, Lutheranism, and the Reformed churches are all in a freefall.

Episcopalianism, once a standard for American religion, cannot get a million people to attend its services on any given Sunday. Several years back, the Episcopal Church was down to sponsoring only 25 foreign missionaries worldwide.[100] As Shiflett says, there are now more lesbians in America than there are Episcopalians.[101]

The Presbyterian Church U.S.A., once one of the most important denominations in America, is also down to a million attendees on any given Sunday. In 2017 alone, they lost more than 67,000 of their 1.5 million remaining members.[102] Disciples of Christ churches, one of the few indigenous denominations in America, have fewer than 300,000 attendees left. The United Church of Christ is down to less than half a million.

At one point, a third of all Americans were Methodist (you read that right). Today, the United Methodist Church can barely get one percent of Americans (three million) in its doors, and as far back as 1998, Thomas Reeves reported that a third of Methodist churches in the U.S. had not performed a single baptism in a year.[103] A 1995 study found that the Methodist Church had been losing a thousand members each week for the past 30 years.[104]

The Unitarian Universalist Association (UUA) can barely get a hundred thousand people in its Sunday services. More people will attend a Tennessee Vols football game on Saturday than the entire corpus of UUA churches the next day. It's no wonder: one UUA leader recently noted more than half of the denomination's members are atheists.[105]

As author Ed Stetzer notes in an article in *The Washington Post*, if liberal Protestantism doesn't change its course, it has only 23 years left.[106] Attendance in mainline—that is, progressive—denominations, has dropped by nearly two-thirds since 1972. And there is no evidence that this decline is about to change. Remember, this is in spite of the flight to such churches by former evangelicals. As the bottom continues to drop out of cultural Christianity in America, even fewer people will be attracted to liberal churches. The future of theological progressivism is dim, as well it should be.

There are various reasons for the demise of mainline Protestantism, but the primary reason is theological liberalism. The message that these churches have preached for nearly a hundred years makes no real claim on its members other than to believe in left-leaning social causes, so eventually the members get it—and just drop out. Further, the constant stream of leftist politics in these churches is often a betrayal of the Christian faith. Those who are serious about historical Christianity are eventually forced to leave the ruins of their churches to find the gospel. Most people need a real reason to get out of bed on Sunday morning. And progressive churches rarely offer one.

All this being the case, it is astonishing how many disillusioned evangelicals—individuals, ministers, and college professors—are drifting toward theological progressivism—some deliberately, but many unwittingly.

It feels like every day I read of Facebook posts from formerly biblical Christians describing their newly-found conversion—away from the sacred treasure secured by the apostles, master teachers, and martyrs and into a value system designed by unbelievers, secularists, and apostates. Sometimes, such conversions are accompanied by stories of "oppression" by evangelical churches, a faux search of the Scriptures for what the Bible "really says," the joining with a new and shrinking community of fellow progressives, and a so-called persecution of the new victim by mean-spirited Bible believers. Missing from these de-conversion stories is any real respect for what biblical Christianity has taught around the globe for nearly two thousand years.[107]

And it feels like every week I get invitations from Christian colleges and universities to come hear another progressive speak *against* orthodox Christianity and *in behalf* of the latest cause of the left. The names of such speakers are largely unknown to the school's supporting fellowships, so members of the churches that built these schools have very little idea just how much their schools have abandoned their founding principles. Many of the professors at evangelical colleges and universities are no longer evangelical or orthodox.

Thomas Oden describes how he pretended to be orthodox while sabotaging the faith:

> In my seminary teaching I appeared to be relatively
> orthodox, if by that one means using an orthodox
> vocabulary. I could still speak of God, sin and salvation,
> but always only in mythologized, secularized and worldly-
> wise terms. God became the Liberator, sin became

oppression and salvation became human effort. The
trick was to learn to sound Christian while undermining
traditional Christianity.[108]

If the typical member of a Baptist church, an Independent Christian church, a Methodist or Catholic church, or an a cappella church of Christ actually knew what was being taught at their own schools, they would likely toss the faculty and administration of its schools overboard.

And members of Bible-believing churches sometimes hear strange sounds coming from their pulpits, as their ministers promote doubt, unorthodoxy, and secular causes in their sermons. Coolness, relevance, and hipness have replaced orthodoxy, holiness, and historical Christian faith in such churches with devastating results. Nothing seems to result in new churches and renewal movements like progressivism, which is increasingly dividing churches and spinning off bewildered members in search of more biblical forms of Christianity.

Let's remind ourselves that we don't have to guess the trajectory of progressivism. Over and over again, two hundred years of theological liberalism have demonstrated that progressivism is not an on-ramp to the Christian faith. Rather, it is an off-ramp that leads to unbelief. I cannot count the number of people I've known who started out with a high view of Scripture, only to lose it at Christian universities from reading progressive authors or by attending liberal churches. These are real people. Real friends of mine. And in virtually every case, they end up in the same place: angry, cynical, and largely agnostic.

I would be remiss if I didn't call out the anger and rage of progressivism. At its heart, progressivism is often a rage against the way things really are. It is often a rage against our gender. It is often a rage against people's natural fallen state. It is often a rage against the natural unfairness of economics, politics, and social structures. It is often a rage against orthodoxy, against rules, and against the establishment. This rage fuels the distinctive need that progressives have for approval—not just acceptance. Progressives insist that others *approve* of their views, celebrate them, and even underwrite them. Indeed, this rage leads progressives to call for punishment of those who don't offer their support of progressivism. In the 1990s, the Episcopal Church was calling for "dialogue" on the question of same-sex marriage. In 2019, they literally punished a diocese that was not willing to perform weddings for them. The constant progressive desire for social revolution is neither healthy nor Christian.[109]

Rage explains why progressives can sometimes be the nastiest people in the city. Progressive gatherings and progressive social media are often marked by protests, screams, censorship, hatred, marginalization, and occasionally even threats and violence.

Here's just one example. In January of 2019, a group of Christian high school students attended a pro-life rally at the mall in Washington, D.C. While there, a group of progressives began to scream at them, subjecting them to racist, homophobic, and bigoted verbal abuse. Then, an older Native American progressive approached one of the boys and started banging a drum in his face. The startled boy kept his cool, and simply smiled back.

Somehow a video clip of a small part of the incident went viral on social media. The way the video was edited made it appear that the boy might have been acting disrespectfully to the Native American. Progressives everywhere went ballistic. Some called for the boy's murder. Others verbally attacked all Christians. The boy's school had to cancel classes because progressives had made so many threats of violence.

And many of these hate-filled rants and threats came from progressive Christians. Rachel Held Evans, who frequently asks the world to "stand up to hatred," went hysterical on Twitter, with multiple tweets about these boys, their school, non-progressive Christianity, the President, masculinity, whiteness, and so forth. Her tweets dripped with hatred.

When it was later proven that the boys were not guilty of anything other than being harassed by progressives, the left generally refused to apologize—including Held Evans.

What makes this all the more astonishing is how disproportionate the accusations were. That same month, the trial of one of the world's most violent drug dealers, responsible for the grisly murder of hundreds if not thousands of people, was revealing the horrors of the world of illegal drugs. Additionally, that same month the state of New York passed a bill declaring all unborn people to be "non-human." All of them could legally be killed from that point forward in New York. The progressive governor of Virginia even suggested that *born* babies could be killed. But there was no rage from Held Evans against these horrors, just against the Catholic boys who crossed her vision of America.

Progressives assume the rightness of their views, so they simply cannot imagine why others are not as enlightened as they. For this reason, progressives have begun a long campaign to ban biblical viewpoints from the public square. They punish businesses that don't support progressivism. They delete accounts on social media that aren't lock-stepped with their agenda.[110] They are beginning to pass municipal laws that criminalize our freedom to *exercise* our religion—the first right of the U.S. Constitution.

Mark my words: when real persecution breaks out against biblical Christians in America, it will be supported, or even led, by progressive Christians who are already writing angry blogs against biblical Christians as well as amicus briefs in favor of discrimination against Christian viewpoints. Screams and angry rants are the blanks a movement uses before firing live ammo.

I am not arguing for conservative politics or for a particular brand of evangelicalism. Like progressivism, conservativism and evangelicalism are particular ideologies. They sometimes get things right, but they also get things wrong. You don't have to vote Republican to be a biblical Christian; there are many times that orthodox Christians must oppose Republican policies and politicians, just as we must often oppose Democratic policies and politicians. Biblical Christianity is not about making America great again—despite the many great things accomplished in and by America. Biblical Christianity is, instead, about inviting people into the kingdom of God.

In fact, though biblical Christians must be firm and unyielding on the gospel, we biblical Christians should also walk humbly. We should be honest about the fact that we have often gotten things wrong. Biblical Christianity can be co-opted, just as progressivism has been, by forces that use it for their own advantage. Many times, Bible-believing Christians have been on the wrong side of matters—one need only recall slavery in the South or the Civil Rights movement of the 20th century. In both cases, Baptist Christians, Christian Church Christians, conservative Methodist Christians, members of the Church of Christ, and other evangelical denominations disastrously undermined their own credibility by twisting Scripture to justify their evils.

Numerous so-called biblical Christians have sometimes perpetrated some of the worst racial sins. I can sympathize with African Americans who are leery of evangelical churches, and I both apologize for our past and am working to make right the wrongs fueled by hundreds of years of abuse. These are cases where we must admit that progressivism was often more biblical than biblical Christianity. Fairness and humility demand that we acknowledge this and that members of biblical churches repent, speak rightly, and even make amends for such past wrongs. To some extent, biblical Christians have undermined our own witness by our lives.

But acknowledging the sins and foibles of biblical Christians does not imply that we should rewrite the faith. We don't eliminate speed limit laws just because people break them. Instead, we repent of breaking the law, strengthen its enforcement, and find ways to protect ourselves from the lies we tell ourselves when we want to speed. When Bible-believing Christians fail to obey the Bible, the proper response is to repent of our sin, make restitution for our failure, and strengthen our resolve. Compromising the Bible because of our failures is *not* the right solution.

The sacred Scriptures really have the right answers, even if we fail to live up to them. Paul makes this very argument in Romans 7:12-16. His inability to live up to the law doesn't mean the law is wrong; instead, it proves why we need the law. If a motorist hits a child while speeding in a school zone, we don't blame the law. We blame the speeder and strengthen the law. And we care for the child injured by the lawbreaker.

When Christians violate their own book, that's not a reason to throw out the book. Rather, we should discipline the Christian, strengthen our resolve to obey the book and care for the victims of disobedience.

Walking in Humility

But what about the tensions in the Bible? Aren't there good reasons for us to be skeptical about some of what the Bible says? To argue the conviction that we return to Scripture is not to suggest that there are no difficulties in the Bible or that following Scripture is simple. There are thorny questions for 21st-century readers of the Bible, and biblical Christianity can be hard and often counter-intuitive.

There are difficulties in the Christian Scriptures. Only a person who has never read the Bible could say it does not have tensions, problems yet unresolved by us, and statements that seem inconsistent with the general flow of even orthodox Christianity. Dealing with the violence of the Old Testament is a problem for everyone, not just progressives.[111] The question of the canon is a legitimate question that requires even biblical Christians to pause and reflect.[112] What the Bible teaches about sex and gender may make sense at some levels, but at other levels it seems odd and needless.

So how do we respond to these paradoxes and questions?

First, we must remember that the Bible presents us with a "take it or leave it" character. It doesn't offer us the option of picking and choosing which parts we'll believe. When we trust Jesus, we trust him "as is," not "as we want him to be." The same is true with the Bible. It's too consistent a book, with far too many pieces dependent upon each other and far too demanding for us to divide it between portions we accept and those we reject. It's like a complicated machine—if one part ceases to work, the whole of it fails. If God didn't speak to Jonah about the big fish, he didn't speak to Jonah about good and evil either. If God didn't authorize Paul to distinguish between gender roles in the church, then God didn't speak to Paul about grace, either. If Jesus was wrong in his predictions about his resurrection, he was also wrong in his teachings about the poor. Have you ever thought that when we pick and choose from the Bible what we will and won't believe, we're guilty of the worst sin—the sin of making God into our image?[113]

If we were unbelievers, we could at least maintain our integrity when we rejected what the Bible says. As a friend of mine once said, "The reason I am not a Christian is because I believe that the Bible actually means what it says. That's more than most Christians believe." I pray for my friend's faith, but I respect his integrity. He believes the Bible means what it says.

Progressives, on the contrary, honestly appear to believe that they are smarter than Moses, more visionary than the prophets, and know Jesus better than did his holy apostles. Many honestly appear to believe they are more spiritual than God. So they are comfortable picking and choosing which parts of the Bible they will embrace, treating entire sections as wrong, or at least as metaphorical. But the Bible really does not give us that choice. The whole stands or falls with each of its parts.[114]

So we must approach Scripture with the determination to reject any hermeneutic that is based on convenience. Once we accept the Christian faith, we accept the Bible—whether we agree with it or not. Again, to use the metaphor of marriage, once you say "I do," you spend the rest of your life seeking ways to live consistent with your vows, even when it's hard or when you don't want to. Once you're baptized, you spend the rest of your life working out the implications of what the Bible teaches, even when it's hard or when you don't want to. Once you are baptized, you are done with "whether or not" questions—questions about whether or not you will believe, whether or not you will obey, and whether or not the Bible is true. Once you're baptized, the questions become "how" questions: How can I trust? How can I obey? How can I purify my heart to accept? The Scriptures have a word for anything less than this: *apostasy.*

Of course, tensions still exist. So the second thing we must recognize when dealing with the paradoxes of Scripture is that our minds are naturally darkened. Christian theology has taught this all the way back: not only is our will in bondage, our minds are also in bondage. John Calvin articulated the concept of original sin in such a way as to underscore just how little we can trust our own minds. By nature, we often fail to love truth. By nature, we often make excuses. By nature, we often justify ourselves, ignore plain evidence, and practice deceit. If we depend solely upon our own minds to understand the Word of God, we are truly throwing pearls before swine. Without the witness of the Spirit, we are hopelessly prone to misunderstanding the things of God. The reason God had to send Jesus was to set us free from the corruption of our minds.

This is why our minds must be saved in addition to our souls. It's why we must avoid those things that tend to play to our lusts, our greed, our passions, and our dark side. This is a primary work of the Holy Spirit, who gives us the Word of God and enlightens our hearts to understand it. So we must embrace the Holy Spirit and trust his witness.

But we must also refuse to feed our minds godlessness. In North America, nothing feeds the dark side of our minds like the entertainment industry. I don't think it's too much to suggest that the movies, TV programs, music, and media we consume are directly related to our inability to judge truth from error, beauty from ugliness, goodness from evil. This is why Christianity has always been counter-cultural.

The church of the first few centuries forbade its members from going to the theater and the games; it understood the power of entertainment to woo us from a holy and rightly oriented life. If you frequent godless entertainment, you can be sure that the God-likeness of the Scriptures will never penetrate your mind. And so when Christians feed on godless entertainment and media, they create a mental environment of hostility toward Scripture and orthodoxy. It's no wonder that pastors and theologians who grew up nursing on pagan media now seek to be relevant by acting like pagans. If you feed on godless material, don't expect to understand God. We become what we condition our minds to enjoy.[115]

We Christians are invited to a different way of thinking—one shaped not by the godless culture around us but instead by the great cloud of holy witnesses around us. When we are baptized, we are invited to join a grand community gathered round the Zion of God. There, we receive the great treasure of the church's pastors and martyrs, prophets and apostles, theologians and mystics. There, we are given a profound heritage that includes Peter and Paul, Irenaeus, Augustine, Jerome, Anselm, Aquinas, Francis, Luther, Calvin, Tyndale, Newton, Bach, Wesley, Wilberforce, Tolkien, Teresa, Ten Boom, John Paul, and many more. *These* are our people—these are the men and women who crafted a comprehensive Christian culture, along with a thousand supporting institutions, that shaped the modern world and still breathe life into the church. Their voices form a living chain back to the ministry of Jesus. In the holy communion of the church, we hear deep whispers that teach us how to read Scripture and, more importantly, how to live it.

If we are to understand and submit to Scripture, it will be necessary for us to live differently—we must "take captive every thought and present it to the Lordship of Jesus" (2 Cor. 12:5) and "renew our minds" as we refuse to conform to the world around us (Rom. 12:1-2). Indeed, we must actually read *the Bible*, rather than merely reading blogs about it. We must be people of prayer rather than of mere play. We will need to restore the ancient disciplines of fasting, simplicity, charity, and meditation. In these disciplines, we open space for the Holy Spirit to enlighten our minds to perceive the meaning of God's Word.

And the Holy Spirit will open the minds of those who want to accept the Word. Paul puts it this way: "Now we have received not the spirit of the world, but the Spirit who is from God, that we might understand the things freely given us by God. And we impart this in words not taught by human wisdom but taught by the Spirit, interpreting spiritual truths to those who are spiritual. The natural person does not accept the things of the Spirit of God, for they are folly to him, and he is not able to understand them because they are spiritually discerned" (1 Cor. 2:12-14).

By avoiding the godless voices around us, by disciplining ourselves spiritually, and by surrounding ourselves with the great cloud of Christian witnesses, we can condition our minds to hear what the Spirit teaches us through the Word. Then, when we live our lives faithfully, our experiences will be interpreted by the Word (rather than the other way around). When we allow the Bible to shape us, we will stop asking the wrong question: "Why should we believe what the Bible says about that?" and can start asking the right questions: "What is wrong with me that I wouldn't want to submit to this teaching?" and "How can I do what it says today?" When we allow the Spirit to lead, the Bible becomes clear.

I pray for a movement of Christ followers who will ask these questions and be moved to act on the answers. I pray that we will produce 21st-century believers who tremble at God's Word.

What Is the Responsibility of the Church?

Back to my days at Vanderbilt (I described my experiences in detail in Chapter 1 and introduced you to Dr. Barrett). Dr. Barrett was a New Testament scholar and visiting lecturer. In a room of progressives, I had engaged him in a question about changing the Christian faith or the Scripture in order to suit our personal beliefs and feelings.

He had tartly responded that the Christian faith isn't open for negotiation.

Immediately after my question, several students whispered their disapproval of his response to me. But I've thought a lot about what this ordained Methodist minister and biblical scholar said that day. A few years before Barrett's career, another brilliant European New Testament scholar had said nearly the opposite. Rudolf Bultmann was a Lutheran theologian and professor of religion at the University of Marburg. Bultmann had immersed himself in mid-20th-century existential philosophy. He was convinced that existentialism was the defining truth of modernity, and he wanted to show that the New Testament was relevant for existentialists.

His problem was, of course, the actual content of the New Testament, which is distinctly unmodern. And so Bultmann sought to save the New Testament by "demythologizing" it. The authors of the Bible were mere interpreters of the experience they had of Jesus, but their experiences were bound up in their limited, pre-scientific worldviews, Bultmann argued. The task of the modern reader, Bultmann argued, is to strip away the forms and expressions of the Greek and Hebrew writers of the Bible and discover their eternal, existential truths.

In Bultmann's hands, virtually everything in the Bible was stripped of its original meaning. He actually followed the same logic as modern progressives: he took the New Testament teachings, declared them "culture bound," stripped away the culture, and left us with nothing but existential platitudes. Bultmann was only different from progressives in the degree to which he exercised his rewrite of the Christian faith. Contemporary progressives suggest the Bible was culture bound in its teachings about gender and sex. Bultmann was much more courageous. He stated that the Bible is culture bound in *everything*. No miracles. No holiness. No resurrection, no Christ—these are all mere cultural expressions that modern Christians should cut out and leave behind. Listening to Bultmann's arguments, one wonders why there would need to be a God at all: after all, isn't even God merely an ancient category for speaking about ultimate realities? Bultmann actually believed he had *saved* the Christian religion, made it relevant, and updated it to fit mid-20th-century biases.[116]

Barrett is far more attractive than Bultmann. You can choose to be a biblical Christian or you can choose to construct your own religion, but you can't choose both. Embrace the apostolic testimony, and you will join that crowd of witnesses around Zion's throne. Marry the spirit of the age, and you will be a widow in the next. Literally, *nobody* today embraces Bultmann's 1950s existential program for reading the Bible—even though in its day, it promised to save the world.

In the middle of the Great Depression, J. Gresham Machen, former professor of religion at Princeton University and co-founder of Westminster Theological Seminary, pondered the rise of theological liberalism. He had fought it himself, and often despaired over its acidic results on students of religion.[117] Only a few years before his untimely death, Machen raised the question of what the future of Christianity must be:

> The responsibility of the church in the new age is the same as its responsibility in every age. It is to testify that this world is lost in sin; that the span of human life—no, all the length of human history—is an infinitesimal island in the awful depths of eternity; that there is a mysterious, holy, living God, Creator of all, Upholder of all, infinitely beyond all; that he has revealed himself to us in his Word and offered us communion with himself through Jesus Christ the Lord; that there is no other salvation, for individuals or for nations, save this, but that this salvation is full and free, and that whoever possesses it has for himself and for all others to whom he may be the instrument of bringing it a treasure compared with which all the kingdoms of the earth—no, all the wonders of the starry heavens—are as the dust of the street. An unpopular message it is—an impractical message, we are told. But it is the message of the Christian church. Neglect it, and you will have destruction; heed it, and you will have life.[118]

Every generation of believers gets to choose who they will be; our generation is no different. Before us stands the choice of life or death. Progressivism will not stand; it has severed itself from everything that made the faith great. That's why every progressive denomination is dying. But the great apostolic tradition has been here two thousand years and it is flourishing around the globe. After two millennia, it is *still* changing hundreds of millions of lives—it *still* offers faith, hope, joy, and love. The apostolic faith will stand until the day Jesus returns—and it will never end.

So like everybody else, you get to choose.

Choose life.

Final Reflections

How Must We Respond to Progressivism?

A friend contacted me some time back and asked for my opinion about the church he had been attending for years. He and his wife were beginning to hear what they called "strange sounds" from their pulpit. Some of the ministers on staff were promoting the works of authors who downplayed biblical truths and emphasized, instead, progressive Christianity. My friends had asked for a meeting with the leadership of the church, but they could not get clear answers about what their church leaders believed about some important matters. Instead, the leaders seemed to stonewall my friend and accuse him of being divisive. The friend eventually left the congregation into which he had poured so much of his time, resources, and heart.

"What else could we have done?" he asked me.

With so many North Americans leaning into progressivism, a lot of us are now being forced to make a decision. What do you do when your minister begins to quote extensively from progressive authors and speakers? How do you navigate family members who are enamored with progressivism? Is there a way for you to determine clearly what constitutes apostolic Christianity?

These are important questions, and ones that can only be answered with courage and long-hauled conviction. Allow me to say a few things briefly that might help you to answer some of these questions.

Read Your Bible

By definition, apostolic Christianity is the Christianity of the Bible. The apostles and prophets of the Scriptures were ordained by God to reveal to us the faith Jesus expects us to have. Many of us are enamored by blog posts, podcast episodes, books, and keynote presentations that talk *about* the Bible and Jesus, but we are lax in our willingness to spend time actually reading the Scriptures. A simple reading of the Bible, consistently, repeatedly and aided by the great interpreters, creeds, and witnesses of the Christian community, can prevent us from falling for many ideas that are simply unbiblical. We become what we hear. If we are hearing everybody except those who are actually entrusted with the Christian message, we will not recognize false and misleading teaching when it is presented.

Allow one example. Many progressives argue that there is simply no place in the Christian life for hatred. It sounds reasonable and just; after all, this world has been marred by enormous amounts of hatred throughout history. So we hear such platitudes as "hate speech is not free speech," or "hate is not welcome here." But if one reads the Bible (and uses common sense), one sees that there are times where hatred is both necessary and just. The hatred of sin is necessary for people who want a better world. The hatred of injustice is God-like and right. Don't progressives hate racism? Don't they hate child abuse? Of course they do. And as I have already mentioned, all one has to do is look at the Twitter feed of various progressives to see a river of rage, hysteria, and hatred.

The God of the Bible is sometimes described as "hating": he hates a lying tongue (Prov. 6:16ff) and robbery (Isa. 61:8), and he stands firmly against those who lift themselves above him (Jer. 50:31). Jesus says that he hates the works of the Nicolaitans—those who teach people to sin sexually or to worship idols (Rev. 2:6, 14-15). If we read closely, we will see that the Bible condemns *unjust* hatred, not all forms of hatred. In spite of the indulgent affirmations of progressives, some hatred is both necessary and healthy.

But you may not ever realize this truth if you don't read Scripture for yourself. Instead, you are likely to fall for the simpleton placards of progressivism, rather than the deep truths of Scripture. Of course, Scriptures often present events, ideas, and actions that are hard for North Americans to hear, but if we allow the Scriptures to teach us, we will develop a healthy view of truth, rather than a distorted and unrealistic view of truth. But you will only know these things if you read your Bible.

Here's a simple exercise for cultivating an apostolic, biblical worldview: read through the Bible and make a list of everything that the Bible teaches that seems to be contrary to the spirit of the age in North America right now. Now we all misunderstand some things, so you cannot rest your final convictions on a short reading of Scripture. But if you see themes in the Bible that are repeated over and over again and then you hear denials of these themes from those you know who are Christians, you'll know for yourself that there's something wrong.

Let the Bible form your ethics, morals, and spirituality. Let the Bible tell you which questions matter most. And let the Bible give you the answers to these questions.

Read your Bible, but don't read it alone. Test your interpretations by submitting yourself to church history, your church leaders, and the all-but-forgotten metric called obedience—which is the most important hermeneutic for any follower of Jesus. Let me tell you what I mean.

Let Obedience Be Your Guide

We as people learn through obedience, but North Americans do not really value obedience. We value, instead, self-affirming "authenticity"— by which we mean doing what you feel is right, then waiting for others to approve it. But obedience is a repeated command of Scripture with which we must reckon. It was Jesus who said, "Whoever believes in the Son has eternal life; whoever does not obey the Son shall not see life, but the wrath of God remains on him" (John 3:36). The theme of obedience runs from cover to cover in Scripture. But what is more, we understand some things in Scripture only through obedience. Obedience is the best hermeneutic.

Some years back, I decided to take a course in karate. It met a couple of times per week, and though I didn't really have the time for it, it was actually one of best things I've ever done. I loved the discipline. I loved the camaraderie.

After moving from white to yellow belt, my sensei began to have us do in karate what's called *kata*. Think of *kata* as a series of carefully prescribed moves something like a dance. Every week we practiced a number of *kata*. As much as I liked karate, I didn't like the *kata*. They seemed to be a waste of time.

Then, when I received my green belt, we were allowed to begin sparring. Suddenly, I realized why we had been doing the *kata* all along. Turns out, the *kata* are exactly the moves you make when you are sparring with someone! In fact, if you simply do the *kata* when sparring, you can actually take out your sparring partner. I questioned why I had to do the *kata* when I was ignorant. But by obeying my sensei, I learned how to spar through those same *kata*. I only came to understand because I first chose to obey.

In the same way, Jesus instructs us that if we want to understand his teachings, we must learn to obey them. The NIV translates John 7:17 as follows: "Anyone who chooses to do the will of God will find out whether my teaching comes from God or whether I speak on my own." If you want to understand Jesus and the Scriptures, learn to obey. It's better than knowing Greek and Hebrew. It's better than podcasts and books. Listen to the Word and obey.

Be Suspicious of North American-Sounding Spirituality

As I mentioned in the early part of this book, every generation tends to interpret the Scriptures in light of their own experience. To some extent, this is inevitable, and we need fresh applications of age-old truths, no doubt. But we should be suspicious when thought-shapers begin to say things that sound very much like the general consensus around us. As I've already said, North American values tend toward the individual, toward sentiment, toward indulgence, toward celebrity-ism. It's a perfect mix for progressivism to flourish.

Celebrities promote some new cause that appears to be "inclusive" or "just" or "compassionate." People begin to signal their alignment through social media. The talk shows pick up the cause, featuring heartbreaking stories of how badly mistreated someone has been. Soon, politicians get on board explaining that the new cause is a "human rights" issue. Finally, Christians "discover" that the latest secular cause has been hiding in the Scriptures for 1900 years, and they have just now discovered it!

Meanwhile, nobody seems to notice how very American the cause is, how un-Christian it might be, and how much the rest of the world is shaking its head at our narcissism, lack of discipline, and unfaithfulness.

Jesus advises us that the world is going to *reject* us because we won't follow along with the latest celebrity causes:

> If the world hates you, know that it has hated me before it hated you. If you were of the world, the world would love you as its own; but because you are not of the world, but I chose you out of the world, therefore the world hates you. (John 15:18-19)

The entire book of Revelation was written to comfort Christians who would not compromise on sexual sin or align themselves with the pagan values of Roman culture. But the book is also a warning to Christians: abandon the biblical teaching on sex and acculturation, and Christ will remove your lamp from his presence (Rev. 2-3).

I know this sounds brash, but it needs to be said: if rich, self-indulgent Hollywood elites are promoting it, there's a really good chance it isn't Christian.

Refuse to Sit under Compromising Teachers

This point is hard, but it must be said. Peer pressure is real—and it's not just for teens. We become like those we hang around. If you allow yourself to be instructed by teachers who are comfortable undermining biblical teaching, at some point your own respect for the apostolic witness is going to be compromised. You know this is true, even if you don't want it to be.

Now, we must practice some nuance here. Nobody fully agrees with your particular understanding of everything. Odds are, even you don't agree with every particular point of theology you have. If you do, you're probably not learning much—our theology should grow, which involves, of course, change. So I am not arguing that you should only learn from people who will tell you what you already believe. Nor am I arguing that you should be afraid to grow in faith and understanding.

But what I am saying is that when you begin to see bloggers, authors, and leaders *deliberately undermine the apostolic witness*, especially when it is done in such suspicious ways as to affirm secular American values, you should go on full alert. When you hear a popular teacher suggest that the Gospel of John is "two steps backward" because it disagrees with his theory of anti-dualism,[119] you are not hearing a different interpretation of John's Gospel. You are hearing a *rejection* of it. You are hearing someone say that they know Jesus better than the one who literally dined with his head next to the heart of Jesus.

Do you really want to sit under this kind of teaching?

If you were to go to a law court over a contract dispute, the judge would rightly tell you that the four corners of the contract constitute the only agreement you have. You can debate what the contract means. But you cannot legitimately say that you want the judge to disregard the contract based on how you *feel* about it. Not if you want a favorable judgment.

In the same way, we humans are going to find ourselves in honest disagreement about what the contract of Scriptures means. We have, after all, fallen minds, and must await the resurrection to know fully the mysteries of God's revelation. Disagreements about what the Scriptures mean can be healthy and necessary. But at the heart of progressivism is the belief that we should go *beyond* the contract of Scripture. At its heart, progressivism isn't just an argument over this or that meaning of a biblical text. It is an argument that we shouldn't be bound by the text at all. Progressives come to court not to receive a judgment regarding the contents of the contract. They come to court to get the contract thrown out.

You'll make your decision, but I wouldn't sit under the feet of people who believe they know more about Jesus than the apostles, the prophets, and in some cases, Jesus himself.

Engage Respectfully, but Be Willing to Walk Away

Back to Alisa Childers. Not too long ago she tweeted a humorous comment her husband made when some book arrived in the mail: "Does this go in the book shelf or the heresy cabinet?"

Of course one reason Alisa's husband can say this is because Alisa actually engages with progressives from a biblical point of view. I highly recommend her website (www.alisachilders.com): she is winsome and respectful but firm. Her book review of Rachel Hollis's book *Girl Wash Your Face* was viewed more than two million times!

Those of us who have committed ourselves to the Jesus of the apostolic witness cannot ignore what progressives are saying. Progressivism will die out one day—just as every liberal denomination is dying, even as I write this. But in the meantime, progressivism is beguiling hundreds of thousands of believers. This is not a time to remain quiet. Rather, it is a time to speak respectfully and honestly about what is going on. It is a time to speak up when we hear leaders dismiss Scripture. It is a time to make it clear to our friends and family that we are not ashamed of the witness of the Bible. It is a time for us to have honest conversations with those who seek to rewrite the faith—not "dialogue" in the sense of negotiating but conversations where we explain clearly the stand we have taken.

This is a time to draw a line in the sand and have the courage to refuse to be cool and hip but instead to be a faithful disciple of Jesus. This is what you meant when you confessed that Jesus is Lord. A confession is not an argument, and it is not a "dialogue." It is not a logical debate. A confession is a statement of resolve. When I first confessed that Jesus is the Christ, the Son of God, the Lord of lords, I was stating my resolve to trust and obey him regardless of what everyone else does, regardless of what *anyone* else does. If the whole world backs down, I'm not going to.

So I suggest that you be willing to discuss respectfully and openly your confession of faith with those who are leaning into progressivism. You likely won't be able to change their minds; you may not even be that good at stating your position (and they may not be good at stating theirs either). But everyone deserves a chance to hear the message of the Jesus of the Bible in love and kindness.

If your church has obviously begun to lean toward progressivism, I recommend you state your position to the church leaders gently and in love. If they are not interested in moving back toward Scripture, I would leave. Life is short. Why spend your time in constant anxiety about what they're going to do next? Besides, progressive churches typically die slow deaths. If they are going to stay the progressive course, you're likely sailing on the Titanic.

Case in point. In 2015, the senior pastor of GracePointe Church in the upscale, Nashville suburb of Franklin announced that the church was going progressive, particularly on matters of sexuality. The move was celebrated by progressives everywhere—it was treated as though it were a turning point in evangelicalism. *Time* magazine even got in on the act, identifying GracePointe as something of a role model for other evangelical churches.

But things didn't go so well for the church. Soon after the announcement, attendance at GracePointe began to drop sharply. When GracePointe announced their change, they were running nearly one thousand people on Sundays. Within a few months, they had lost half their membership. One visitor two years later said he couldn't count two hundred and fifty people who were left.[120] Contributions also dropped sharply as members left in search for more biblical expressions of the faith. Soon, GracePointe was laying off staff. Then, a little over a year ago, the church was forced to put its building on the market due to lack of funds. They moved to Nashville, where they now share a building with another progressive congregation. Then, in late 2018, the senior pastor who brought the changes to GracePointe announced his own departure. It's unclear what the future of GracePointe will be, but progressive churches like this rarely grow—and sometimes crash like this one did.

Remember this: typically, when a congregation begins to go progressive, it also begins a long, slow death. You don't have to stay at such a church. But if you do decide to leave, I would do so in such a way as to avoid splitting the church. There has been enough division in Christian history. Leave lovingly and humbly. Don't leave grumbling and gossiping. Then, find a church where apostolic Christianity is held in high esteem.

Whatever you do, pray for everybody involved. Who knows what Christ will do if we pray? Eventually, people will get tired of progressivism. Deep down inside, most of us want the real thing.

In the closing years of the late 18th century, one could easily have guessed that Christianity was on its way out in the U.S. Elites were tending toward deism rather than biblical Christianity. Thomas Paine's *Age of Reason*, with its challenge to the Christian faith, was one of the most popular books in America. On the frontiers, whiskey, gambling, and adultery were more important than the Christian faith. Church attendance was in decline.

Then, in June of 1800, at a little log cabin church in Logan County Kentucky, a small revival broke out. The little church there had been praying and fasting for a revival for years. Its leader—a serious revivalist preacher named James McGready—had been challenging people to commit fully to God and respond in complete repentance. One night, a few members actually took him seriously. A tiny revival broke out.

Before long, word of the revival spread across Kentucky and Tennessee. By 1801 a friend of McGready's named Barton Warren Stone had decided to host his own revival. The rest is history: as many as 20,000 people showed up for the Great Cane Ridge Revival—a tenth of the state of Kentucky. From Cane Ridge sprang hundreds more revivals across the South. Soon, such denominations as the Baptists, the Methodists, the Christian Churches, and Presbyterian Churches were sprouting everywhere, and in those days, all of them had a very high view of Scripture. The Methodist Church went from fewer than 30 congregations in the U.S. at the outbreak of the Revolutionary War to more than 20,000 by the Civil War—all in the span of one lifetime.

I believe God will do it again. He honors those who honor his word. He wants his Word to go out into the world. He wants us to be faithful to Jesus—not the Jesus we invent but the Jesus who is. But even if we don't see such a revival in our lifetime, Christ is still in charge. And he *will* get his way.

And when he does, you'll want to be standing by his side.

About the Author

DAVID YOUNG completed an M.A. at Harding School of Theology and an M.A. and Ph.D. in New Testament at Vanderbilt University. He has worked for churches in Missouri, Kansas, and Tennessee, taught at several universities, and spoken around the world. He is the host of the New Day Television Program and author of several books, including *The Rhetoric of Jesus in the Gospel of Mark* (Fortress Press, 2017) which he co-authored with Michael Strickland. David currently serves as the senior minister for the North Boulevard Church of Christ in Murfreesboro, Tennessee. David and his wife Julie have two married children. David is a co-founder of Renew.

Endnotes

1. Jen Hatmaker, *A Modern Girl's Guide to Bible Study: A Refreshingly Unique Look at God's Word* (Colorado Springs: NavPress, 2006), 14.

2. I'm indebted to Renée Sproles for the language here. See *On Gender: What the Bible Says about Men and Women and Why It Matters* (Renew, 2018), 13-14.

3. Most progressives prefer the term "progressivism" to the term "liberalism" for several reasons. First, the term "liberalism" has negative connotations for many Americans, who are by instinct rather conservative people. Second, the term "liberalism" implies "liberty," and could be construed to mean such things as small government—as in libertarianism—while virtually every progressive wants larger government. Perhaps the biggest reason that many prefer the term "progressivism" is because it can include people who are not full-blown theological liberals but are merely on the way out of evangelicalism and orthodoxy. "Progressivism" is a broader word than "liberalism" and allows room for people who are closer to Scripture than say the episcopal establishment. In this book, I generally use the term "progressivism" to include both those who are moving away from biblical Christianity, as well as full-blown liberals. I have attempted to limit my use of the term "liberalism" to describe those who have fully embraced the canons of developed liberalism.

4. https://www.huffingtonpost.com/entry/nadia-bolz-weber-purity-ring-vagina-sculpture_us_5bfdac5ee4b0a46950dce000, accessed January 11, 2019.

5. Rob Bell, *Love Wins* (New York: HarperOne, 2011).

6. Richard Rohr, "Incarnation Instead of Atonement," https://cac.org/incarnation-instead-of-atonement-2016-02-12/, accessed October 21, 2018.

7. Shane Claiborne and Tony Campolo, *Red Letter Revolution: What If Jesus Really Meant What He Said?* (Nashville: Thomas Nelson, 2012).

8. *Inspired: Slaying Giants, Walking on Water, and Loving the Bible Again* (Nashville: Thomas Nelson, 2018).

9. See http://www.theliturgists.com/.

10. Former evangelical Bart Ehrman actually raises a question similar to this in a blog post on his personal website: "Why Even Bother Being a Liberal Christian?" https://ehrmanblog.org/why-even-bother-being-a-liberal-christian, accessed July 30, 2018. Ehrman's answer seems to be something like, "I just need a tribe."

11. Lesslie Newbigin, *Foolishness to the Greeks* (Grand Rapids: Eerdmans, 1988), 64.

12. At this point, I must say something about the term "orthodoxy." I know that it is a slippery term and one that is the subject of numerous concerns. Without getting into all the specifics, by "orthodoxy" I mean historic forms of Christianity that are consistent with the great truths of Scripture, generally embraced by the main streams of historic Christianity, taught by the great Doctors of the Church, and put forth in the major creeds and confessions. Certain forms of Christianity have been rejected by almost all Christians; these I consider either heterodox or heretical or both.

13. Jen Hatmaker, *7: An Experimental Mutiny Against Excess* (Hatmaker Partners, 2017), 92.

14. Some of what I witnessed while at Vanderbilt is also chronicled in Thomas C. Reeves's *The Empty Church* (New York: Free Press, 1996), especially pages 166 and following. My guess is that some of what Reeves reports would embarrass even progressives today.

15. The sources for progressivism are vast, covering two hundred years. Perhaps the most comprehensive history of theological progressivism is Gary Dorrien's superb three-volume work, *The Making of American Liberal Theology* (Louisville: John Knox Press, 2001, 2003, 2006). See also Conrad Wright, *The Beginnings of Unitarianism in America* (Berkeley: Starr King Press, 1955); J'annine Jobling and Ian Markham (eds.), *Theological Liberalism: Creative and Critical* (London: SPCK, 2000), Randall Balmer and Lauren Winner, *Protestantism in America*, Columbia Contemporary American Religion Series (New York: Columbia University Press, 2005); and Ismail Kurun, *The Theological Origins of Liberalism* (Boston: Lexington Books, 2016). Critiques of theological progressivism also abound. For a sampling, see Thomas C. Reeves, *The Empty Church: The Suicide of Liber-*

al Christianity; R. R. Reno, *In the Ruins of the Church* (Ada, MI: Brazos Press, 2002); Dave Shiflett, *Exodus: Why Americans are Fleeing Liberal Churches for Conservative Christianity* (New York: Sentinel, 2005); John Nugent, *Endangered Gospel: How Fixing the World is Killing the Church* (Eugene, Oreg.: Cascade Books, 2016); and James Heidinger, *The Rise of Theological Liberalism and the Decline of American Methodism* (Franklin, Tenn.: Seedbed Publishing, 2017).

16. Progressivism remains largely a white, middle and upper-class movement, even though it often embraces issues and concerns of non-white, non-aristocratic persons. The early founders of American theological progressivism were often overtly white racists—as were, of course, many of their evangelical counterparts. Indeed, the father of modern American theological liberalism, Horace Bushnell, argued that African Americans were so inferior to whites that they stood in the way of American progressive ideals (see Dorrien's *The Making of American Liberal Theology*, vol. 1, 128ff). Bushnell was also anti-Semitic and anti-Catholic. White culture is native to theological progressivism, since progressivism is, at its heart, a civic religion engineered for an English population by white, East Coast gentry. So for example, the liberal PCUSA reported in 2005 that 97 percent of its membership is white. Compare that with evangelical churches, which report only 76 percent white membership (David Olson, *The American Church in Crisis* [Grand Rapids: Zondervan, 2008], 160). The old slur WASP (white, Anglo-Saxon Protestant) was originally used to describe progressives, not evangelicals.

17. See the recent Pew Research study that showed that African Americans have a considerably higher view of the Scriptures than white, elite Protestants. See http://www.pewresearch.org/fact-tank/2018/05/07/blacks-more-likely-than-others-in-u-s-to-read-the-bible-regularly-see-it-as-gods-word/, accessed December 23, 2018.

18. See Dorrien, *The Making of American Liberal Theology*, vol. 1, 318ff.

19. I say "exempting only themselves" not to be mean-spirited or cynical. All of us are probably hypocritical at some level, but in my experience, progressives sometimes take hypocrisy to new levels: building walls around their homes while protesting the building of border walls; flying first-class while railing against fossil fuels; buying every new gadget while calling for the dismantling of free markets; arguing for increased funding for public

education while sending their children to elite private schools, etc.

20. See also Jon H. Roberts and James Turner, *The Sacred and the Secular University*, The William G. Bowen Memorial Series in Higher Education (Princeton: Princeton University Press, 2000).

21. This tendency to make the phrase "the kingdom of God" into a social gospel goes back to the work of early progressives. Walter Rauschenbusch explicitly advocated for a social interpretation of Scripture in the early 20th century, becoming the "father of the social gospel." But in recent decades, the emphasis on the kingdom of God as a social program has been largely popularized by such theologians as John Howard Yoder and the enormously influential N. T. Wright. Yoder made popular Mennonite readings of the Bible, which emphasized Jesus over Paul and the Sermon on the Mount as a social program. Wright has advocated a Jesus who had a social view of the kingdom of God as opposed to a Jesus who advocated personal salvation—heaven is "God's space on earth" as much as it is the place to which the saved go when they die. Both Yoder and Wright have offered valid and, at times, necessary corrections to evangelicalism. But in the hands of many of their followers, Christianity has often devolved into little more than a social reform movement, showing itself as left-leaning evangelicals seeking to "build God's kingdom here."

22. This misuse of ink color has actually become something of a cottage industry among progressives. Tony Campolo articulates the group's thesis in his book *Red Letter Christians: A Citizen's Guide to Faith and Politics* (Grand Rapids: Baker Books, 2008). There he argues that we should center our faith on the red letters of the Synoptic Gospels. But typically, his use of red letters turns out to mean little more than a support for the latest platforms of left-leaning politics. Most "Red Letter Christians" ignore the red letters of Jesus in the Synoptics about hell, exclusion, and judgment. Further, most "Red Letter Christians" actually *disagree* with the red letters in the Gospel of John and in the Book of Revelation, as the red letters in these books fail to align with the Jesus progressives are trying to construct.

23. Scotty McLennan, *Jesus was a Liberal* (New York: St. Martin's Press, 2009), viii.

24. See Rod Dreher's *The Benedict Option: A Strategy for Christians in a Post Christian Nation* (New York: Sentinel, 2017).

25. Considered as a percentage of the U. S. population, liberal Protestantism is

equally small. According to David Olson's research, only three percent of Americans attend a mainline Protestant church. See *The American Church in Crisis* (Grand Rapids, MI: Zondervan, 2008), 54. More than nine percent of Americans attend an evangelical church any given Sunday, 57.

26. Peter Enns, *The Bible Tells Me So: Why Defending Scripture Has Made Us Unable to Read It* (New York: HarperOne, 2014), 65.

27. The following quotes come from Mary Poplin's *Is Reality Secular?* (Downer's Grove: Intervarsity Press, 2014) and "The Unlikely Conversion of a Radical Scholar," The Well (online) https://thewell.intervarsity.org/focus/unlikely-conversion-radical-scholar, accessed July 18, 2018.

28. The problem goes back to the early 19th century and the work of Ralph Waldo Emerson. The earliest progressives argued for reason over revelation. Emerson moved beyond reason and suggested that imagination is a better source for theology than reason. For Emerson the romantic, the beauty of the Christian faith lay in the ability of theologians to turn it into "the human spirit writ large." See Dorrien, *The Making of American Liberal Theology*, vol. 1, 45ff. Since Emerson, imagination unhinged from Scripture has become an important concept in progressive circles.

29. https://myemail.constantcontact.com/Daily-Meditation-God-Is-Never-Less-Loving-Than-the-Most-Loving-Person-You-Know-Foundation-March-4-2013.html?soid=1103098668616&aid=tnw6_ojTXqA, accessed January 3, 2019.

30. A recent Pew Religion and Public Life study surveyed 443 Episcopalians and found that 47 percent of them say the Bible is not the Word of God. This is a truly astonishing number, though less astonishing when you consider the same survey indicates that only 19 percent of Episcopalians say they get their sense of right and wrong from their religion. The survey can be found at http://www.pewforum.org/religious-landscape-study/religious-denomination/episcopal-church/racial-and-ethnic-composition/, accessed August 3, 2018.

31. It is worth noting that in the Synoptic Gospels Jesus rarely uses the word grace, and certainly does not use it in the sense one typically hears today. Grace is a Pauline concept. The theology of Christian grace that progressives love is absent from the Bible if one does not accept Paul.

32. Peter's claim in this text was likely directed at Gnostics, who argued that Jesus was not really human. But the statement eerily presages the work of

many theological progressives today, who try to demythologize the Bible. Peter is clear: he is not writing a myth; he is writing an historical fact.

33. A quote from T. S. Elliott's poem, "The Wasteland," referencing Augustine's sexual appetite as a young student of rhetoric in North Africa.

34. https://www.mlive.com/living/grand-rapids/2015/02/rob_bell_on_gay_marriage_were.html, accessed January 5, 2019.

35. https://www.christianitytoday.com/ct/2010/december/9.25.html, accessed November 28, 2018.

36. Unless one is prepared to argue, as I am, that the entire Bible is the work of Jesus.

37. This is explicitly claimed by Papias, who knew at least one apostle. Quoted in Eusebius, *Ecclesiastical History*, 3.39.15.

38. It may be a more egregious form of ignorance, since Peter was actually discipling Mark shortly before Mark wrote his Gospel (1 Pet. 5:13). The Peter who wrote adamantly about holiness and sexual purity in 1 Peter is the same Peter who taught Mark the red letters in Mark's Gospel. It requires dramatic ignorance to pit the Jesus of the Synoptics against the rest of the New Testament.

39. There are numerous versions of this hermeneutic; Webb's is originally found in his work *Slaves, Women, and Homosexuals* (Downer's Grove, IL: Intervarsity Press, 2001). Webb nobly seeks to distinguish between culturally bound teachings and timeless truths, and he tries to be conservative in the application of his method. But those who use his method frequently end up merely judging Scripture based on contemporary Western sensibilities. Webb himself seems to lower the standards in his subsequent book against corporal punishment, *Corporal Punishment in the Bible: A Redemptive-Movement Hermeneutic for Troubling Texts* (Downer's Grove, IL: Intervarsity Press, 2011). See the responses to Webb by Wayne A. Grudem, "Review Article: Should We Move Beyond the New Testament to a Better Ethic? An Analysis of William J. Webb, Slaves, Women and Homosexuals: Exploring the Hermeneutics of Cultural Analysis," *JETS* 47 (2004): 299–346, and Benjamin Reaoch, *Women, Slaves, and the Gender Debate: A Complementarian Response to the Redemptive-Movement Hermeneutic* (Phillipsburg, NJ: P&R Publishing, 2012).

40. It is also true that there are trajectories of biblical application for Christians and the Word of God. Indeed, the applications of the Bible to our

social contexts will always require renewal and reformulation. But this is not the same as suggesting that the very truthfulness of what the Bible says is open to a supposed trajectory.

41. Tim Keller, *The Reason for God* (London: Penguin Books, 2008), 115f. Cf., C. S. Lewis's argument against what he called "chronological snobbery," i.e., the belief that your particular time and place knows more than any other.

42. Tim Keller, *The Reason for God*, 75.

43. Marcus Borg says in *The Heart of Christianity*, "The notions of biblical infallibility and inerrancy first appeared in the 1600s and became insistently affirmed by some Protestants only in the 19th and 20th centuries" (New York: HarperCollins, 2003), 12.

44. See, for example, Augustine's statements regarding infallibility: "I confess to your charity that it is only to those books of Scripture which are now called canonical that I have learned to pay such honor and reverence as to believe most firmly that none of their writers has fallen into any error. And if in these books I meet anything which seems contrary to truth, I shall not hesitate to conclude either that the text is faulty, or that the translator has not expressed the meaning of the passage, or that I myself do not understand," *Letter to Jerome* (405), 1:3.

    The doctrine of the infallibility of Scripture is implicit in the creeds too. For example, The Westminster Confession of Faith says, "The whole council of God concerning all things necessary for his own glory, man, salvation, faith, and life, is either expressly set down in Scripture or by good and necessary consequence, maybe deduced from Scripture unto which at any time nothing is to be added whether by new revelations of the spirit or traditions of men" (3.6).

45. Reno notes that the church father Origen viewed such problems in the Scriptures as a deliberate pedagogical tool used by God to lead us to further study. For this reason, Origen could wrestle with the tensions of Scripture at the same time that he believed every single word of it. See Reno, *In the Ruins of the Church*, 140ff.

46. Theological progressives have changed views on numerous positions through the years, sometimes supporting, then opposing, the exact same view with equal passion. Early on, theological liberalism stood staunchly against Catholics, Jews, and Muslims, before declaring religious bigot-

ry wrong and treating Muslims as a persecuted minority. There is still a strong anti-Semitism among many progressives. Liberalism started out as a promotion of white, Whig values, with not a few founders openly racist. Today, white elites enjoy their elitism at the same time that they rail against white privilege. Progressivism once opposed abortion as a social evil, before turning abortion rights into the liberal equivalent of the virgin birth. Progressivism was once against alcoholic consumption, before voting to repeal the 18th amendment. It was against gambling, before it supported state-sponsored lotteries. It was against same-sex behavior and transgenderism, which it defined as mental illnesses, before it declared both of these healthy self-expressions that should be promoted by the government. Even core liberal values from the past are being eaten alive by contemporary progressives—concepts such as freedom of speech and association, the objectivity of science, and the dangers of massive government. Liberalism originally meant freedom; today it means massive bureaucracy, policy-driven ethics, and statism.

47. Robert Cialdini, *Influence: The Psychology of Persuasion* (New York: Collins Business, 1984), 129.

48. Rosaria Butterfield notes the role that obedience served in her conversion: "I've discovered that the Lord doesn't change my feelings until I obey him. Obedience comes before understanding," *The Secret Thoughts of an Unlikely Convert: An English Professor's Journey Into Christian Faith,* 2nd edition (Pittsburgh: Crown & Covenant Publications, 2014), 22. She references John 7:17, which posits a hermeneutic of obedience: "If anyone's will is to do God's will, he will know whether the teaching is from God or whether I am speaking on my own authority."

49. Malcolm Muggeridge, *Jesus Rediscovered* (London: Fontana, 1969), 24-25.

50. As quoted in Dinesh D'Souza, *Conversion of a Cynic*, https://www.crisis-magazine.com/1984/conversion-of-a-cynic, accessed July 18, 2018.

51. https://johnpavlovitz.com/2016/12/07/the-beautiful-activist-heart-of-jesus/, accessed January 11, 2019.

52. It is not hard to see how liberals can go from assuming that Jesus' death was a mistake to believing that much of his life was mistaken too. Such distrust of Jesus has often been hidden beneath the surface of progressivism. At least the progressive luminary Theodore Parker (d. 1860) was honest when he said, "It is vain to deny, or attempt to conceal, the errors

in [Jesus'] doctrine—a revengeful God, a Devil absolutely evil, an eternal Hell, a speedy end of the world." Quoted from "A Discourse of Matters Pertaining to Religion," in Dorrien, *The Making of American Liberal Theology*, 99.

53. https://www.youtube.com/watch?v=4LYQQO5uFtA, accessed January 11, 2019.

54. *Saving Jesus From the Church: How to Stop Worshiping Christ and Start Following Jesus* (New York: HarperCollins, 2009), 92.

55. Richard Rohr, "Incarnation Instead of Atonement."

56. Arminianism forms the main Protestant alternative to Calvinism. The latter asserts double predestination—that God predestines some for heaven and others for hell. This form of predestination essentially renders free will irrelevant. For advanced Calvinists, those destined for hell must sin. Arminianism asserts that humans have a natural tendency to sin, and all will eventually sin, but that we possess the freedom of will to avoid sin. Presbyterians are Calvinist. Methodists are Arminian.

57. Augustine, *Confessions*, 2.9-14.

58. It's worth noting that liberal optimism also fails to bring real satisfaction. Rather, it brings frustration and, many times, clinical depression—these are evidences that we know we aren't good.

59. A classic on the Pelagian Controversy is still the introduction entitled: "Augustine and the Pelagian Controversy" composed by B. B. Warfield in *From Nicene and Post-Nicene Fathers*, Series I, Volume V.

60. Solzhenitsyn, *The Gulag Archipelago* (New York: Harper and Row, 1973), 168.

61. A summary of some contemporary theories can be found in *The Nature of the Atonement: Four Views*, eds. James K. Beilby and Paul R. Eddy (Downer's Grove, IL: Intervarsity Press, 2006). For a contemporary defense of the classical doctrine of atonement, see Scot McKnight, *Jesus and His Death: Historiography, the Historical Jesus, and Atonement Theory* (Waco, TX: Baylor University Press, 2005) and John Stott, *The Cross of Christ* (Downer's Grove, IL: Intervarsity Press, 2006).

62. The Westminster Confession of Faith, 11.3.

63. Joseph Priestly (1733-1804), a founder of British Unitarianism, went so far as to say that there is no trace of Jesus' divinity in the Scriptures. Priestly listed many criticisms of historic Christianity in his *An History of the Cor-*

ruptions of Christianity (1782). He influenced early American theological liberalism, especially with his doctrine of the mere humanity of Jesus and his denial of the atonement.

64. Regarding universalism, see the exciting new book by Michael McClymond, *The Devil's Redemption: A New History and Interpretation of Christian Universalism* (Ada, MI: Baker Publishing Group, 2018). McClymond demonstrates that universalism is completely incompatible with both the Bible and historical Christian theology. Universalism is another gospel.

65. Cf., Steve Chalke and Alan Mann, *The Lost Message of Jesus* (Grand Rapids: Zondervan, 2003), 182-183. Brian McLaren makes the term popular, suggesting that the doctrine of atonement renders God a child abuser. McLaren could only mean this if he didn't believe that Jesus is God.

66. Some of the material that follows is from my time spent with Annie in behalf of her ministry, "Hookers for Jesus." Most of it, however, can be found in her autobiography, *Fallen: Out of the Sex Industry and Into the Arms of Jesus* (Nashville: Worthy Publishing, 2015).

67. Lobert, *Fallen*, 152.

68. Lobert, *Fallen*, 153.

69. Kim Phuc, *Fire Road* (Carol Stream, IL: Tyndale, 2017), 110.

70. https://www.npr.org/2016/10/14/497804739/in-a-jail-sentence152a-veterans-redemption-with-help-from-a-fellow-vet, accessed July 31, 2018.

71. *Finding God in the Waves: Why I Left My Faith and Found It Again through Science* (Convergent Books, 2016), 201.

72. J. Herbert Kane, *A Concise History of Christian World Mission*, (Ada, MI: Baker Academic, 1978), 7.

73. See the important work of Matthew Bates, *Salvation by Allegiance Alone* (Ada, MI: Baker Academic, 2017), which demonstrates that the gospel includes the present kingship of Jesus and the need to live loyally to King Jesus. See also Scot McKnight, *The King Jesus Gospel: The Original Good News Revisited* (Ada, MI: Brazos, 2016).

74. Bates, *Salvation by Allegiance Alone*, 47.

75. Bates, *Salvation by Allegiance Alone*, 52 *ad passim*; italics are Bates's. Bates borrows from the work of C. H. Dodd, *The Apostolic Preaching and Its Developments* (New York: Harper & Row, 1964), 17.

76. See the transcript of McLaren's statements at https://reformed-nazarene.wordpress.com/emergent-church-what-is-it/brian-mclar-

en-the-cross-as-false-advertising/, accessed January 12, 2019.

77. Matt. 5:22; 5:29; 5:30; 10:28; 16:18; 18:9; 23:15; 23:33; Mark 9:43; 9:45; 9:47; Luke 12:5.

78. Malcolm Muggeridge as quoted by Ravi Zacharias in *Jesus Among Other Gods* (Nashville: W Publishing Group, 2002), 153.

79. K. P. Yohannan, *Revolution in World Missions* (Carrollton, TX: GFA Books, 2009), 106.

80. Sociologist Rodney Stark points out how, in the opening centuries of the church, apostolic Christianity brought justice to the world: "Christianity served as a revitalization movement that arose in response to the misery, chaos, fear, and brutality of life in the urban Greco-Roman world .... Christianity revitalized life in Greco-Roman cities by providing new norms and new kinds of social relationships able to cope with many urgent problems. To cities filled with the homeless and impoverished, Christianity offered charity as well as hope. To cities filled with newcomers and strangers, Christianity offered an immediate basis for attachment. To cities filled with orphans and widows, Christianity provided a new and expanded sense of family. To cities torn by violent ethnic strife, Christianity offered a new basis for social solidarity. And to cities faced with epidemics, fire, and earthquakes, Christianity offered effective nursing services .... For what they brought was not simply an urban movement, but a new culture capable of making life in Greco-Roman cities more tolerable," Rodney Stark, *The Rise of Christianity* (Princeton: Princeton University Press, 1996), 161.

81. See the statement by Kevin DeYoung, "Is Social Justice a Gospel Issue?" https://www.thegospelcoalition.org/blogs/kevindeyoung/social-justice-gospel-issue/, accessed September 16, 2018: "As far as we know, the term 'social justice' dates to the 1840s when it was first used by a Jesuit philosopher named Luigi Taparelli (1793-1862). Taparelli was a strong supporter of papal authority and a conservative Catholic who argued that social inequality is not a violation of justice but a byproduct of justice, which he understood to be the right ordering of constitutional arrangements. Taparelli's use of 'social justice' bears little resemblance to how the term is used in common conversation today."

82. The triclinium of the Roman world required that men lie on their sides as they ate, so it wasn't uncommon for men to be next to each other's chests during meals. But John is nearly named "he who reclines against Jesus,"

showing a holy and intimate relationship.

83. http://www.vergenetwork.org/2011/09/14/mike-breen-why-the-missional-movement-will-fail, accessed August 21, 2018.

84. Ibid.

85. For those readers who are young, this is not a made-up illustration but is exactly what the Episcopal Church did in 2003 with bishop Gene Robinson.

86. Carl F. Henry, *Confessions of a Theologian* (Nashville: Word Books, 1986), 270.

87. Malcolm Muggeridge, https://www.goodreads.com/quotes/4488213-jesus-himself-even-in-his-obscurity-dreaded-thegathering-of.

88. Many social activists exhibit symptoms of issue-attention-deficit disorder. This explains why they change out social justice concerns every five or ten years. Yesterday social activists opposed prostitution, alcohol, population explosion, climate cooling (yes), racial mixing, and censorship. The *New York Times* and every mainline Protestant denomination once stood firmly against abortion. Today, progressives are mum on the problems of pornography, while distilleries and small batch breweries are enjoyed by progressives as a sign of urbanity everywhere. Climate change is now about warming, and social activists are the new censors. Instead of racial eugenics, progressives have named racism the original sin while often hurling racist rants against whites. Today, Protestant denominations and the Gray Lady advocate government-funded abortions. There's a fickleness to liberal progressivism that betrays its seriousness as a philosophical system. In any case, isn't there at least some chance the issues that concern well-bred Ivy League and Hollywood upperclassmen are different from those that drive followers of Jesus?

89. Cf., the first-person testimony of Hollywood writer-producer Ron Austin, regarding how much the entertainment elites were willing to turn blind eyes to the evils of socialism in the 1950s and '60s. "Blacklisted," *First Things* (March, 2018), 9-12. Joy Davidman, the eventual wife of C. S. Lewis, explains her early fascination with atheistic communism in the same language—she deliberately blinded herself to the evils of socialist utopianism because she wanted her ideology to be true. In a moment of honesty, however, she let God in, and he changed her forever. The story of her conversion is well told by Trevin Wax, *This Is Our Time* (Nashville: B

& H Publishing, 2017), 53ff.

90. *Tread Softly for You Tread on My Jokes* (New York: Harper Collins, 1966). For a bizarre example of this, consider the experience of John Azumah, Professor of World Christianity at Columbia Theological Seminary. Azumah tells about a class he taught in his Introduction to Islam course at Columbia. The ordained Presbyterian minister from Ghana had invited an Imam to come in to speak to his class. According to Azumah, the Imam denied that Jesus was the Son of God, denied that Jesus was crucified, and maintained that the Bible had been falsified. Azumah says that the mostly Christian students politely listened and seemed rather bored. They asked various questions, but none was very hard. Finally, someone asked the question about Islam and homosexuality. When the Imam answered by saying homosexuality is un-Islamic, not of God, and unnatural, the faces of students grew red with shock and rage. They got very angry and began to argue. Azumah says that this was his first introduction to American Christianity—that denying Jesus is the Son of God is acceptable but questioning homosexuality is not. See "Through African Eyes: Resisting America's Cultural Imperialism," *First Things* (October, 2015).

91. J. D. Vance, *Hillbilly Elegy: A Memoir of Family and Culture in Crisis* (New York: Harper, 2016), describes his upbringing in a dysfunctional family cursed by the collapse of America's sexual and religious ethics. He recalls some of the adverse childhood experiences children like him have endured: being sworn at, insulted, or humiliated by parents; being pushed, grabbed, or having something thrown at you; feeling that your family didn't support each other; having parents who were separated or divorced; living with an alcoholic or a drug user; living with someone who was depressed or attempted suicide; watching a loved one be physically abused. One quote from Vance says a lot. When he was nine, his mother and her third husband moved the family away from his beloved grandparents. Soon, the marriage of his mother and her husband began to deteriorate into violent fighting matches. He writes: "I began to do poorly in school. Many nights I'd lie in bed, unable to sleep because of the noise—the furniture rocking, heavy stomping, yelling, sometimes glass shattering. The next morning, I'd wake up tired and depressed, meandering through the school day, thinking constantly about what awaited at home …." He gained weight and developed PTSD. Progressivism got what it wanted—moral unrestraint.

Millions have suffered as a result.

92. See the penetrating insights of R. R. Reno, *Resurrecting the Idea of a Christian Society* (Washington: Regnery Books, 2016). "Today's 'progressive' is committed to expanding lifestyle freedom, which the rich tend to manage, like economic freedom, to their advantage. But while the benefits of economic freedom do in fact extend even to the poor, what trickles down from lifestyle freedom is dysfunction, disorder, and disarray," 41. "The weapon of mass destruction in our war on the weak has been moral relativism, heedlessly deployed by an elite culture in love with critical strategies for disenchanting old, inherited moral norms," 50. Reno depends heavily upon the social assessments of Charles Murray, *Coming Apart: The State of White America, 1960-2010* (New York: Crown Publishing, 2012).

93. David T. Moore, *Five Lies of the Century* (Carol Stream, IL: Tyndale House, 1995), 89-90.

94. Hubbard, *Love into Light* (Bingley, U.K.: Emerald House Group, 2013), 139.

95. Put in terms of Paul's teaching on justification, we do good not to be saved, but because we are already saved. This is the argument of Romans 1-8 and is succinctly stated by Paul in Ephesians 2:8- 10: "For by grace you have been saved through faith. And this is not your own doing; it is the gift of God, not a result of works, so that no one may boast. For we are his workmanship, created in Christ Jesus for good works, which God prepared beforehand, that we should walk in them."

96. Thomas Oden, *A Change of Heart: A Personal and Theological Memoir* (Downer's Grove, IL: Intervarsity, 2014), 133ff.

97. Oden would later say, "My life story has had two phases: going away from home as far as I could go, not knowing what I might find in an odyssey of preparation, and then at last inhabiting anew my own original home of classic Christian wisdom," *A Change of Heart*, 140.

98. Oden, *How Africa Shaped the Christian Mind: Rediscovering the African Seedbed of Western Christianity* (Downer's Grove, IL: IVP, 2010).

99. Ibid.

100. Reeves, *The Empty Church*, 13.

101. Shiflett, *Exodus*, 41.

102. https://www.pcusa.org/news/2018/6/4/pcusa-membership-decline-slows-does-not-stop/, accessed August 1, 2018.

103. Reeves, *The Empty Church*, 13.

104. Shiflett, *Exodus*, xv.

105. Shiflett, *Exodus*, 59.

106. Stetzer, "If it doesn't stem its decline, mainline Protestantism has just 23 Easters left," *The Washington Post*, April 28, 2017. Accessed online, July 24, 2018.

107. Cf., the brilliant article by Michael J. Kruger, "The Power of De-Conversion Stories: How Jen Hatmaker is Trying to Change Minds About the Bible," at https://www.michaeljkruger.com/, February 5, 2018, accessed July 31, 2018. Kruger gives five steps used by progressives for legitimizing their de-conversion from biblical Christianity: Step #1: Recount the Negatives of Your Fundamentalist Past. Step #2: Position Yourself as the Offended Party Who Bravely Fought the Establishment. Step #3: Portray Your Old Group as Overly Dogmatic While You Are Just a Seeker. Step #4: Insist Your New Theology Is Driven by the Bible and Not a Rejection of It. Step #5: Attack the Character of Your Old Group and Uplift the Character of Your New Group.

108. Thomas C. Oden, *A Change of Heart: A Personal and Theological Memoir*, 81.

109. I suggest re-reading 1 Peter 2:11-3:7. There, the inspired apostle and first follower of Jesus reminds us that the tools of our witness do not include constant political activism, but rather submission, goodness, and holiness. This world is not our home, Peter says, so we should live here as mere sojourners.

110. An example of this comes from one of my friends and colleagues, who put up on his Facebook page the thrilling story of how the gospel had helped a woman become comfortable with the gender God had assigned to her. Within days, Facebook had deleted and barred the post. Remembering that the term "liberal" means "freedom," one has to wonder how liberalism became so very un-liberal.

111. For an excellent treatment of the problem of violence in the Old Testament, see Paul Copan, *Is God a Moral Monster? Making Sense of the Old Testament God* (Grand Rapids, MI: Baker Books, 2011).

112. A helpful book for considering questions of the canon of Scripture, its sources, and editorial history is *In Defense of the Bible: A Comprehensive Apologetic for the Authority of Scripture*, by Steven Cowan and Terry Wilder

(Nashville: B & H Academic, 2013).

113. As Tim Keller says, "Now, what happens if you eliminate anything from the Bible that offends your sensibility and crosses your will? If you pick and choose what you want to believe and reject the rest, how will you ever have a God who can contradict you? You won't! You'll have a Stepford God! A God, essentially, of your own making, and not a God with whom you can have a relationship and genuine interaction. Only if your God can say things that outrage you and make you struggle (as in a real friendship or marriage) will you know that you have gotten a hold of a real God and not a figment of your imagination. So an authoritative Bible is not the enemy of a personal relationship with God, it is a precondition for it," *The Reason for God*, 118. Oden describes the process by which he ignored Scripture in his early life: "My previous relationship to Scripture had been a filtering process that permitted those sources to speak to me only insofar as they could meet my conditions, my worldview and my assumptions as a modern person," *A Change of Heart*, 147.

114. This does not mean that the Bible does not use metaphor. It does. But the question one should ask when considering whether or not a text is metaphorical is whether or not a text would conflict with another text if taken literally. Progressives use a different standard: they take a text to be metaphorical whenever that text conflicts with their sensibilities. We should remind ourselves that Scriptures are multi-textured, but at the end of the day, they mean what their authors intended them to mean. Authorial intent is the controlling factor in reading the Bible. See the works of E. D. Hirsch, *Validity in Interpretation* (New Haven, CT: Yale University Press, 1967) and Kevin Vanhoozer, *Is There a Meaning in This Text? The Bible, the Reader, and the Morality of Literary Knowledge* (Grand Rapids, MI: Zondervan, 2009).

115. One is tempted to say that such mental conditioning is the spiritual equivalent of the doppelganger effect—a well-known experiment in which a person has his left hand covered up and a rubber hand set in its place. The experimenter brushes both the right hand and the rubber hand. Eventually, the subject of the experiment begins to "feel" the brush on the rubber hand. Apparently, the brain must accommodate the information it is being fed, and it literally changes its perception of reality. If we feed our minds godlessness over and over again, our minds will eventually begin to feel

that godlessness is good.

116. My Ph.D. dissertation was largely a challenge to Rudolph Bultmann's method of interpreting the Gospels and has now been updated by my friend and colleague Michael Strickland and published by Fortress Press. See David Young and Michael Strickland, *The Rhetoric of Jesus in the Gospel of Mark* (Minneapolis: Fortress Press, 2017).

117. J. Gresham Machen's criticism of theological liberalism is still relevant. See *Christianity and Liberalism* (1923).

118. J. Gresham Machen "The Responsibility of the Church in Our New Age," *Selected Shorter Writings*, ed. D. G. Hart (Phillipsburg, NJ: P & R Publishing, 2004), 376.

119. Richard Rohr, https://peteenns.com/a-contemplative-look-at-the-bible-with-richard-rohr/, accessed January 3, 2019.

120. https://juicyecumenism.com/2017/11/09/gracepointe-church/, accessed December 18, 2018.

Made in the USA
Monee, IL
23 September 2022